HOLDING ON TO ROMANCE

HOLDING ON TO ROMANCE

KEEPING YOUR MARRIAGE ALIVE & PASSIONATE
AFTER THE HONEYMOON YEARS ARE OVER

H. NORMAN WRIGHT

Regal Books
A Division of Gospel Light
Ventura, California, U.S.A.

Published by Regal Books
A Division of Gospel Light
Ventura, California 93006
Printed in U.S.A.

Scripture quotations in this publication are from the following versions:
NIV, The Holy Bible: New International Version. Copyright © 1973, 1978, 1984 by the International Bible Society. Used by permission of Zondervan Bible Publishers.
TLB, The Living Bible, Copyright © 1971 by Tyndale House Publishers, Wheaton, Illinois. Used by permission.
KJV, The Authorized King James Version.

Originally published as *Romancing Your Marriage.*

Library of Congress Cataloging-in-Publication Data

Wright, H. Norman.
    [Romancing your marriage]
    Holding on to romance : keeping your marriage alive and passionate after the honeymoon years are over / H. Norman Wright.
        p. cm.
    Originally published as: Romancing your marriage. 1987.
    Includes bibliographical references.
    ISBN 0-8307-1527-4 (hardcover)
    1. Marriage—United States. 2. Love. 3. Marriage—Religious aspects—Christianity. 4. Interpersonal relations. I. Title.
    HQ734.W94955 1992
    306.8'1—dc20

                                                                                        91-47722
                                                                                        CIP

1 2 3 4 5 6 7 8 9 10 11 12 13 14 15 / QE3.0 / KP / 99 98 97 96 95 94 93 92

Rights for publishing this book in other languages are contracted by Gospel Literature International (GLINT). GLINT also provides technical help for the adaptation, translation, and publishing of Bible study resources and books in scores of languages worldwide. For further information, contact GLINT, Post Office Box 488, Rosemead, California, 91770, U.S.A., or the publisher.

Contents

Preface   7

1. Romance—Where Did It Come From?   11

To help us understand romance, let's look at how society's attitude toward it has developed over the years.

2. Romance—How Do You Define It?   25

Romanticism does not always imply a sensational setting or erotic physical activity.

3. No Intimacy? No Romance!   45

Your spouse cannot know you unless you invite him or her into
your inner world.

4. Love? What Is It?   65

Love in marriage...is an unconditional commitment to an imperfect
person.

5. Where Did the Romance Go?   85

As the rains of reality and the winds of stress blow upon the
dream-world marriage, the relationship that was to last "forever"
quickly crumbles.

6. Ridding Your Romance of Resentment   103

Holding resentment toward your spouse will keep you living in
the past, contaminate the present, and limit the possibilities of the
future.

7. Prospering in the Midst of a Love Recession   117
Unlike the victim of a financial recession, you are never bankrupt
of currency in a love recession.

8. Learning to Speak Your Spouse's Language   141
Your romance, love and intimacy hinge on you and your spouse
becoming bilingual.

9. Rejoice in Your Sexuality!   169
The Scriptures encourage the enjoyment and sensual delights of
sex within the boundaries of a marriage relationship.

10. Creative Ways to Keep Your Romance Alive   193
Now and then you may need to reach outside your own idea
bank for some new romantic strategies.

Conclusion   217

Exercises and Quizzes for   223
Keeping Your Romance Alive

Study Questions for
Individuals, Couples and Groups   229

Preface

hen Romancing Your Marriage *was first launched in* 1987, I felt a deep longing to see it used as a tool to reignite the flickering flame of love that seemed to be so prevalent among frustrated couples, many of whom were at the point of giving up all hope.

Now, five years later, I'm encouraged to see that many couples' relationships are growing as they seek help in rekindling their dying romance. I'm especially encouraged when I hear that the material in this book has been part of that rekindling process. How exciting to see the spark of hope, which originally caused these couples to begin seeking help for their relationships, turned into reality, to hear the testimonies of love renewed and marriages healed.

Maybe that's where you are today—seeking help for a dying relationship. Maybe that's why you've picked up this book. If so, let me encourage you to take the time to read through these pages. Let me challenge you to work through the easy, fun, enlightening exercises. (I'll even give you tips on how to get that reluctant spouse involved.) And then let me rejoice with you as you begin to see life and hope and love revived in your marriage.

~ O N E ~
Romance– Where Did It Come From?

*T*he slightly overweight, middle-aged brunette sat across from me in my office, nervously twisting her wedding ring as she related the all-too-familiar story of faded dreams and dying romance.

Once high school sweethearts who couldn't bear to be apart from one another for more than a few hours at a time, Frank and Jan seldom spent any time together anymore except to sit—he in his favorite recliner, she on the couch—watching mindless TV reruns all evening until one of them flicked off the set and headed for the bedroom. The other would soon follow, but seldom with romance in mind. If there was any sexual activity between them, it was perfunctory at best. Most of the time, however, there was nothing more than a "good-night" peck on the cheek, before turning their backs to one another. In minutes, Frank would be asleep, snoring softly, while Jan stared silently into the darkness.

"It hasn't always been like this," she said, as if trying to convince me even as she reminded herself. "I mean, in the beginning, it was wonderful—most of the time, anyway. And then the kids came and we were so busy working and taking care of them, and...well, I didn't really notice anything was wrong until recently. But now that the kids are getting older and will soon be leaving home, I wonder what I'll have left when they're gone?"

She sighed and dropped her eyes. "I don't mean to sound so ungrateful," she said. "I know I have so much to be thankful for—a nice home, great kids, a hard-working husband...."

Her voice trailed off and she looked back up as tears filled her eyes. "But sometimes...sometimes it's just not enough. Sometimes I wish...I wish things were like they used to be—when we were young. We used to have so much fun together then. We'd laugh and talk for hours. We went everywhere together. But now..."

The tears spilled over onto her cheeks, as she shook her head dejectedly. "Now it seems we have nothing in common but the kids and bills. I never thought it would be this way. I expected so much more."

She shrugged her shoulders. "I don't know. Maybe this is normal. Maybe it happens to everybody and I should just accept it. But...deep down, I just can't believe that. I just can't believe that God puts two people together in a lifelong relationship, only to have the love and romance die out in the first few years."

Leaning forward in her chair, she fixed her eyes on me pleadingly. "Am I wrong to expect more?" she asked. "Will it always be this way, or should I hang on and hope for something better?"

In my many years as a professional counselor, I have heard that same longing expressed, time and again, from frustrated, love-starved people, sincerely seeking a renewal of lost romance and intimacy in their relationships. Usually, it is the woman who seeks help first—but not always. Men, too, long for romance and intimacy in their marriage, but most aren't able to identify, much less express, that need.

But in answer to Jan's question, "Should I hang on and hope for something better?" I answer with a resounding "Yes!" However, I must add one thing: A healthy, loving relationship requires more than hoping—it requires ongoing effort and attention.

And that's what this book is all about. While I can confidently say that renewed romance and intimacy is possible in any marriage, a couple must be willing to take a long, hard look at their relationship, and at themselves as well. I have attempted to help you do that through a combination of information, illustrations, and user-friendly quizzes and exercises.

Of course, it is best if both husband and wife work through this

---

Today we appear to have an obsession with romance that some would call pathological.

---

book together; however, if you find your spouse is reluctant to cooperate, don't push or nag. Just go ahead and start reading alone. As you come across interesting tidbits, you might comment, "Gee, did you know that...?" or "Have you ever heard about...?" I call those kinds of questions "teasers." After making your comment, do not elaborate. Just leave the question hanging in the air and go on with your reading. Sooner or later, curiosity is going to get to your spouse and you will find him or her reading over your shoulder.

Another great approach to draw in your spouse is what I call a "grabber" statement. A great example of that is, "Wow, I just came across a prayer about sex in chapter nine. Let me read it to you." Chances are you'll meet with little resistance. However, after you've read the prayer aloud, unless your spouse pursues a discussion on the topic, drop it and continue reading. As I just said, you won't be reading alone for long.

Like Jan, some of you may have a difficult time envisioning your seemingly disinterested spouse becoming interested enough in rekindling your dying romance to actually get involved in working through a book like this. But deep down, each of us has a need to be loved and cherished, and, yes, even romanced on occasion. Your problem is nothing new—it's been around since the Garden of Eden. But dying romance does not have to be a terminal disease. There is hope! Read on—and be encouraged.

What Is Romance Anyway?

Men and women have been falling in love for thousands of years and stories of romantic love have always captured our attention. Romance has produced great music and literature, and has inspired painting and sculpture. Through the centuries courting behaviors and romantic styles have changed among the various cultures of our world. Today we appear to have an obsession with romance that some would call pathological.

What is romance anyway? Is it something tangible we can hold in our grasp? Or is it as fleeting as a fantasy? To help us define romance, let's look at how society's attitude toward it has developed over the centuries. From this overview perhaps you will discover your own style of romance.

Animal Magnetism

Have you ever observed a romantic animal? No, I'm not talking about human romantic animals like Don Juan. I mean an *animal* animal! Perhaps you've never considered animals as being romantic. I guess I didn't either. Yet animals do have their own styles of courtship behavior. And I find some of these styles quite similar to those of us humans.

In the world of the black widow spider, the male is considered the wimp of the species since his mate is four times larger than he is. Furthermore, only the female is glossy black; the male is white and gold.

When the male comes to court his big black beauty, he does so very carefully. Though blind, the female is a sensitive, deadly huntress who knows every inch of her web by touch. The male plucks at the web deliberately like a troubadour plucking a love song on a guitar. This constant rhythm calms the female and she awaits her lover's approach. Every few steps he plucks again so she won't respond as though he is just another insect caught in her web. Finally he reaches her, strokes her with his delicate front legs and the mating process begins.

After mating, the male spider is exhausted and, in his weakened condition, often stumbles about the web as he tries to leave. These irregular vibrations trigger the female's hunting instinct. She not only slays her mate—thus earning her popular title—but devours him as well.

Unfortunately, the black widow's pattern of behavior has a similar counterpart in human relationships. There are many ways by which men and women dominate or abuse their mates, effecting a slow, sure death of the marriage. Romance and intimacy are among the first elements to wither in the "assassination" of a spouse.

The pied hornbill is an exotic bird with an enormous beak. When it is time for the hornbills to mate, the male looks for a hollow tree to convert into an apartment. After mating, the male drives the female into the tree and seals her inside by covering the entrance with mud. Talk about male domination! His mate is not allowed outside until the young are ready to leave the nest. Everything the family needs is shoved into the apartment by the male through a small opening he has left for that purpose. Interesting! I've seen some similarities of this style somewhere else.

Rattlesnakes have a very intense but brief, erotic relationship. When the male finds a female during the mating season, he rises above her to his full stature and sways back and forth in a form of ballet. She responds similarly and they quickly entwine. The male then takes off, never to see his mate again. The female carries the young and gives birth, and the babies are on their own from that moment.

In contrast to the creatures above, there are some animals, such as penguins and wolves, who are committed to one mate for life.[1] But enough about animal romance. What about people and their styles of romance?

Cultural Styles of Romance

There are some very different (and strange) courtship and marriage customs throughout the world that either reflect the presence of romance or the total lack of it. Picture yourself in one of these settings and imagine how you would respond.

If you were an Olembra tribesman in Africa and wanted to be mar-

---

The fierce, emotional passion of heterosexual love was not really known until about the twelfth century in the so-called courts of love.

---

ried, a wife could be purchased for four dogs. What does that say about human worth?

In the Komti caste of Ballalpur, India, a girl is purchased in the marriage market at the rate of 100 rupees for each year of her age. But when she reaches the age of ten, she is considered old and worthless and she is available free to anyone who wants her. What would this do to your self-esteem?

If you were a man interested in taking a bride on the island of Saint Kilda in the Hebrides, Scotland, you would have to undergo a grueling premarital test. Before marrying your fiancé, you must climb atop Lover's Rock and stand on one leg at the edge of a jutting precipice. The problem is that the cliff is 850 feet above the Atlantic Ocean and few who slip survive the fall.

In the Upper Nile Valley, the Acholi tribe have a strange courtship custom that may have some merit. Women must marry their husbands three times before the contract is considered legal. The three successive ceremonies are designed to protect men from making hasty decisions.

You may consider these customs strange. But what would these people say about our customs for courtship and marriage? Would our romantic rituals be any less strange to them?

Romance in History

How did the idea of romance develop? How did we come to court the way we do in our culture? Are we simply the product of Harlequin romances and Hollywood movies with no sense of reality?

The first indications of a concept of romance occurred about the same time as the birth of Christ. Ovid, in 2 B.C., wrote a lengthy instructional poem, *The Art of Love*. From Ovid's perspective, love was by nature a conquest. As far as we know, his poem was the first textbook on methods of flirting, attracting lovers, and seduction—and it was filled with details! Ovid educated an entire generation in the techniques of romantic love.

In the following centuries, very little is known about the presence of romantic love. Marriages continued to be arranged by families for reasons of economic, social, or even political convenience. The fierce, emotional passion of heterosexual love was not really known until about the twelfth century in the so-called courts of love. Perhaps the chivalric romances written at that time were the original Harlequin romances!

As courtly love developed, women holding the status of nobility were regarded as ideal romantic objects. Their favors could be won by masculine vitality and bravery, which in turn secured the man's virtue and status. His love was expressed through honor, courage, self-sacrifice, contempt for worldly goods and even for life itself. This is how the mystique of romantic love began to develop. Womanhood was perfected through natural feminine weakness and beauty, and manhood was perfected by adoring, protecting and serving a woman. The games of romantic liaisons were born in the age of chivalry.

The courtly style of romantic love added an imaginative new dimension to male and female roles. Up to that time, relations between men and women were dull and strictly utilitarian. Then love became supersensual. More than just sexual lust, relationships took on a personal quality that had never before been achieved. But this type of love demanded sufficient leisure in which to fantasize, daydream and play the love games. Therefore the common people, who put all their energies into work simply to exist, did not engage in romantic pursuits. Such leisure games were reserved for a small segment of the people—the aristocracy.[2]

During the twelfth century, an extremely influential book was written by a French cleric named Andre the Chaplain. Andre was summoned by the Countess Marie of Champagne to the court at Poitiers to prepare a manual on courtly love. Poitiers had become a haven for troubadours, but many of them lacked refinement. Marie wanted a manual to draw men away from the excitement of hunting, fighting and gaming so that they would become enamored with women. In other words, she wanted them to stop acting so macho and start acting like amorous gentlemen!

The subsequent book, *The Art of Courtly Love,* became the rage of the age and one of the major cultural documents of its time. It was a code of conduct that pushed aside the importance of marriage and established the importance of romantic love. This work continues to impact us today. Even though the basic ideas of courtly love have been modified over the centuries, the Countess's philosophy of romance still affects the way men and women relate to each other today.

Does it surprise you to learn that our romantic ideas are so old, many of them based upon infidelity and extramarital involvement? Countess Marie was attempting to bring some culture to a group of men, many of whom were rude and mannerless. Our common view of romantic love comes straight from this epic book of male manners! Historian Warren Hollister gives us a precise description of the impact of the Poitiers tradition:

> It was from {the romantic love tradition of} Southern France that Europe derived such concepts as the idealization of women, the importance of gallantry and courtesy, and the impulse to

embroider relations with man and woman with potent emotional overtones of eternal oneness, undying devotion, agony and ecstasy.[3]

What instructions were in this manual? What ideas did it suggest? Here are several statements excerpted from the "code of love" as proclaimed by the Countess of Champagne in 1174:

Marriage is no good excuse against loving (that is, loving someone other than one's spouse).

No one can bind himself to two loves at once.

No one, without abundant reason, ought to be deprived of his own love.

No one can love unless urged thereto by the hope of being loved.

Love that is known publicly rarely lasts.

An easy conquest renders love despised, a difficult one makes it desired.

A new love makes one quit the old.

If love lessens, it dies speedily and rarely regains health.

The man prone to love is always prone to fear.

Real jealousy always increases the worth of love.

The true lover thinks naught good but what he believes pleases the co-lover.

Love can deny love nothing.

The least presumption compels the lover to suspect evil of the co-lover.

This famous code then declares:

We pronounce and decree by the tenor of these presents, that love cannot extend its powers over two married persons; for lovers must grant everything, mutually and gratuitously the one to the other without being constrained thereunto by any motive of necessity; while husband and wife are bound by duty to agree the one with the other and deny each other nothing. Let this judgment, which we have passed with extreme caution and with the advice of a great number of other ladies, be held by you as the truth, unquestionable and unalterable.[4]

A very strange characteristic of courtly love was incompleteness. The incomplete romance usually consisted of the distant adoration by a man of a married woman. And much of the essential adulterous passion was expressed within the confines of poetry and fantasies rather than in a physical relationship. The distance and fantasy added a dimension of intense passion since, as we know, it is difficult for any man or woman to compete with the fantasized ideal we hold of them.

Thus, much of courtly love went unrequited, but men and women accepted those conditions. Even though love might not be returned—or in the case of an affair, could not last—the predicament only added to the excitement and passion of the newfound love.[5]

Another characteristic of courtly love that played a major role in the medieval mind was constancy. During these centuries, society looked upon a person who was inconsistent—wavering in his desires and attitudes—as much less than ideal. But an individual who retained an unswerving dedication to his pursuits was thought to exemplify the best quality of life. Constancy was actually a spiritual goal or ideal.

Those who displayed constancy in romantic love were admired and praised. Often a gentleman's love was directed toward a lady who was remote or unavailable to him. But he continued his service to her. His constancy was reflected in the perseverance of his unrewarded loving acts. And even though he suffered from unrequited love, his undying persistence earned him the adoration of his peers. So a person was applauded for loving without expecting anything in return. What a far cry from the attitudes and expectations of today!

For a while courtly love was limited to the select aristocratic few and was frequently interrupted by the social turmoil of the Hundred Years War and the religious crusades. But at the beginning of the seventeenth century, when peaceful and prosperous times again allowed ample room for leisure and social games, romantic love began to flourish like never before. The rising middle class in Europe soon began to emulate the aristocracy and romantic love came to the common man.

In time the tradition of romantic love as a prelude to marriage became well established, but it did not happen overnight.[6] Many literary

Today's films and books abound with a kind of moonlight-and-roses optimism. This trend reflects our culture's emphasis on instant gratification.

influences contributed to the widespread acceptance of romance. The Italian poet Dante, one of the most influential writers of the late Middle Ages, wrote *The Divine Comedy.* This widely read work, and others of Dante's writings, grew out of his obsession for Beatrice, for whom he maintained a fervent but unrequited passion throughout his life.

William Shakespeare devoted his energies to several versions of the romantic myth including the poem, *Venus and Adonis,* and the plays, *Antony and Cleopatra* and *Romeo and Juliet. Romeo and Juliet* is a clear example of how interference with love can actually intensify its passion.

In seventeenth century France booksellers rejoiced whenever a new volume of unrequited love was released. They couldn't keep books of tragic romance in stock! In 1774 Goethe's *Sorrows of Young Werther* impacted all of Europe with its romantic despair. The book described in veiled terms Goethe's unhappy fascination with the fiancée of one of his friends.

Richard Wagner's operas reflect the romantic view of his day. The heroes of four of his works—Lohengrin, Tannhauser and Tristan, Isolde and Parsifal—were medieval knights. Their stories of unconsummated love and heroic devotion were treated at length in ancient legends.

Stories enhancing the mystique of unrewarded romantic love continue to the present day. Two of the most popular American films of all time center on the theme of unrequited love. The tragic affair of Scarlett O'Hara and Rhett Butler is the basis of *Gone with the Wind.* And in *Casablanca,* the impossibility of a love relationship with Mister Rick echoes the same theme. Viewers are still enthralled by romantic relationships in which the attainment of intense passion is ultimately frustrated. Amazing!

The Romantic Trend Shift

Most recently, the tragic motif in romantic literature has been dramatically turned about. For the first time in over 800 years the most popular view of romance is nontragic. Today's films and books abound with a kind of moonlight-and-roses optimism. This trend reflects our culture's emphasis on instant gratification. The idealistic, happily-ever-after view of romance is a form of unrealism and escapism.

Not long ago a Los Angeles TV station ran a special news report on new romance videos hitting the market. The report stated that the new videos, produced by women, were outselling those produced in the past by men. Why? Because women are the primary audience for romance stories. Women know what women like. And women like romance to be more subtle than explicit. They want a sense of mystery. The new videos captured the essence of romance and mystery that women seek.

Look at the success of the paperback romance stories that sell millions each year. Harlequin Enterprises is the industry leader and produces over 200 romance novels each year. British novelist Barbara Cartland has become the central figure among writers of romantic retreats from reality. Mrs. Cartland has sold over 100 million volumes since she began writing in the 1930s.

The modern romance story has a predictable formula. Usually a young, virginal heroine finds herself in an exotic locale, caught up in a "web of deceit and intrigue." Her counterpart is a quiet, brooding, mysterious male stranger. A "chemistry" develops between them, she encounters some danger, he rescues her and they fall into each other's arms discovering they have loved each other all along. The conclusions of these stories usually suggest that any misunderstanding that existed between the two lovers has evaporated and their newfound passion will flourish unchanging forever.

For centuries the theme of European romance was obstructed constancy. Lovers could never get together. Now the theme has switched to constancy. Modern romance implies that passion will remain stable and uninterrupted until the world comes to an end.

Furthermore, today's romances offer the best of both worlds. True love can experience the intense passion from the uncertainty of a developing relationship, but also enjoys the peace of mind promised by a permanent and unchanging relationship. The new emphasis today is "fantasy within the realm of possibility."[7] Would you like to see what I mean? Here is the closing line of one such novel by Mrs. Cartland, *The Dangerous Dandy,* written in 1974: "Then he drew her closer still, he swept her away into a Heaven where they were part of the Divine, no longer two people but one, through all eternity."[8]

Most of us recognize the unrealistic aspect of so many of these stories. Yet we have been influenced by these themes that tend to provoke unrealistic expectations for our own relationships. For those who find very little love or romance in a relationship, the fantasy escape of romantic novels provides some fulfillment even though it is only a tentative state of mind. But these escapes also intensify the pain of the unpleasant relationship since the contrast between real life and the story is underscored. No "hero" in real life can compete with the love heroes in romance stories. And the availability of the escape route often hinders a person from changing what can be changed in his or her life and relationship.

Romance of the type described in this chapter relies upon sustained romantic peaks. But, in time, anything new becomes old and excitement diminishes. Eventually the mountaintop passion of romantic love is weakened and finally exhausted by time itself. Once the constancy in the relationship begins to fade, there is rapid backward momentum, which frightens the participants. If the romantic passions were extremely dramatic and overpowering, the diminishing loss of such will be dramatic and overpowering as well. Soon lovers recognize that, in reality, the object of their romantic desire does not match the ideal, perfect person constructed in the mind.

The variable, unpredictable and unstable character of romantic love produces two qualities: excitement and fragility. But for those romantics who are realistic, the disillusionment does not have to be catastrophic. Many couples realize that intense romance will fade. But instead of despairing, they say to each other, "What will the next stage of our love relationship be like? We know that it will be something deeper, more solid and stable, and that's all right. We won't cling to 'the way we were,' but set our sights on what new elements will develop. Oh, there will be times of romance and excitement, and they will probably be different from what we experience now. But the difference adds a new sense of excitement for us. There is something awaiting us in the future. Something different."

Notes
1. Gary Richmond, Evangelical Free Church of Fullerton, CA.
2. Dwight H. Small, *How Should I Love You?* (San Francisco: Harper and Row Publishers, Inc., 1979), adapted from pp. 9-19.
3. C. Warren Hollister, *Medieval Europe: A Short History* (New York: John Wiley & Sons, Inc., 1968), p. 239.
4. Nathanial Branden, *The Psychology of Romantic Love* (New York: Bantam Books, Inc., 1968), p. 27. Used by permission.
5. Ari Kiev, *How to Keep Love Alive* (San Francisco: Harper and Row Publishers, Inc., 1982), adapted from pp. 6-11.
6. Small, *How Should I Love You?*, adapted from pp. 18,19.
7. Kiev, *How to Keep Love Alive,* adapted from pp. 12-15.
8. Kitty Bean Yancey, "Welcome to the Age of Romance," *USA TODAY*, February 14, 1983.

~ T W O ~
Romance–
How Do You
Define It?

*I*n all my years of counseling, I doubt that I've ever heard two identical definitions of romance. Marian, a widow for six years, had recently remarried. When I asked her for a definition of romance, she answered with a description of how she felt about her new husband the first time they met.

"When I walked into the room, his magnetism surrounded me like a whirlwind! There was something about him that made my heart leap toward him. His eyes captivated me and I knew he was the man for me, now and forever."

Is this romance?

Marian's new husband, Jason, felt much the same way. "I was drawn closer to her every time I was with her. There was something special we had together that defies description. Everything took on a different and special meaning when we were together. And when I wasn't with her, I thought about her constantly. Life is just different because of her."

Is this romance?

Benny and Theresa have been married for over forty years, have four grown children and nine grandchildren. And yet, after all those years together, they were anxious to offer their own definition of romance.

"We like to sit side by side in front of the fire and look through our picture albums from the past 40 years together. We don't say much, but we enjoy these special moments that hold a wealth of memories

Romance is composed of fantasy, emotion, nonrational delights—something different from the ordinary. It is a special time or event for two individuals.

from four decades of togetherness. It's a special time of closeness for us that others may not understand."

Is this romance?

John and Rita have only been married for three years, but they too have their own special definition of romance. "We hike together one weekend each month. We put on our 50-pound packs, head for the mountains and hike through the forest until we get above the timberline. It takes several hours, but there is nothing like it. We stand on the cliffs, tired and sweaty with our arms around each other. We drink hot chocolate and watch the changing colors on the mountain peaks. Few couples ever enjoy this type of companionship and closeness. I wouldn't trade it for anything."

Is this romance?

Yes! Yes! Yes! Yes! For each couple, this is romance. And here is something we must keep in mind: romance means something different to every person.

Have you ever tried to define romance? The subject of romance is very difficult to reduce to one precise definition. Several years ago I decided to settle the issue by going to the dictionary to find the correct definition of romance. I expected Mr. Webster to give me the clarity I was seeking. But I was disappointed.

Webster defines romance as, "An emotional attraction or aura belonging to an especially heroic era, an adventure or calling; to exaggerate or invent detail of incident; to entertain romantic thought or ideas."[1] Does this definition capture the essence of romance for you? It didn't for me either!

The word "romantic" also has a multitude of meanings, including, "Having no basis in fact, imaginary; marked by the imaginative or emotional appeal of the heroic, adventurous, remote, mysterious or idealized; an emphasis on subjective emotional qualities; marked by or constituting passionate love."[2]

Romance is difficult to define because it is not a science or an art form. Romance is composed of fantasy, emotion, nonrational delights—something different from the ordinary. It is a special time or event for two individuals. What is romantically special to one couple may not be so to another.

There are quiet times of romance and there are romantic highs during which lovers feel more alive, full of music and poetry, and life takes on new colors and meaning. For those who desire constantly to live at the ecstatic upper levels of romance, disappointment will be their companion. For those who realize that the intensity of romance varies and that romance periodically recedes for a rest and then returns, satisfaction will be their reward.

Here is how one man describes his experience of romance from the perspective of his older years:

> I happen to be married to a marvelous woman, and we've been together enough years to know that there will be more passionate love on some days than on others. Feelings of romance usually come in trickles rather than in downpours, and once in

awhile there is a drought when it disappears for awhile. But we do not panic, and we both have learned to cherish the minor ecstasies available on any given day. Like the quiet contentment of a Saturday lunch on our patio, when we linger in the sun to talk and she reaches across the table to squeeze my hand. Or an evening spent reading before the fireplace when, if we do not have a lot to say, it is enough to be together.[3]

Webster may be able to help us with some of the technical elements of the definition of romance, and in this chapter I will make a few more attempts at defining and describing this elusive quality. But, practically speaking, your personal definition is probably as valid as any in print.

To get you started pinning down your own definition of romance, why don't you get out a pencil and work through the following exercise. As I mentioned in chapter 1, it is better if you and your spouse can work through these exercises together, but if your spouse is unwilling, go ahead and start on your own. But don't forget to drop a few "teasers" and "grabbers" along the way. Chances are that, sooner or later, your reluctant spouse will join you.

"Romance: A Novel Idea," is the first of many exercises and quizzes designed to help you assess where you are in your romantic relationship; to help you determine where you want to go as a couple, and to show you how to get there; to allow you to have fun as a couple, while working together to improve your relationship.

Ready? All right, let's begin.

Romance: A Novel Idea

Let's try an experiment in romantic thinking. Imagine that you have been asked to write a romantic novel for a major publisher. You have been given complete freedom to create the characters, the plot and the title. Complete the instructions for your best-selling novel in the spaces below:

1. Describe the man and woman in your novel.

2. State the plot of your novel in one or two simple sentences.

3. What is the title of your best-selling novel?

4. Write the opening lines to this novel. Let your thoughts run wild and be creative!

Now let's see how your novel compares to the abundance of romance novels on the market. Here are some titles I found in the bookstore and library: *Honeymoon, Love's Tender Promise, Perfume of Arabia, Unlikely Lovers, Buccaneer Bride, Mysterious Stranger, Once More with Passion, Captive Bride, Sweet Surrender, Shadow of Desire, My True and Tender Love, Outlaw Hearts.*

And here are the summaries taken from the back covers of a couple of romances:

> *Savage Heart:* His blood ran hot with desire...when Tall Cloud first gazed upon stunning Christa Martin. The lustrous waves

of her golden hair blinded him to his own Indian maidens. The leaf green sparkle of her alluring eyes pleaded that he take her to his mats. Though it was forbidden to marry the white-skinned beauty, the handsome young chief was determined to make her his own—whether she consented to it or not!

Her pulse went wild with passion...when Christa first saw the hard sinewy frame of Tall Cloud. The message in his eyes terrified her—but made her run into his arms. The power of his muscles made her tremble but she clung even closer to his strength. The untouched vixen tried to fight the rush of wild desire that surged through her veins. Then his lips claimed hers and she sought only to melt her own aching, yearning flesh to his brazen heart.[4]

The Spanish Rose: He was her family's bitterest enemy...and now he stood before her, his magnificent body in chains, captured by her brother—enslaved. But from the moment ravishing Maria Delgato gazed into Gabriel Lancaster's burning emerald eyes there was no question who was the real prisoner....

Gabriel despised this tempting Spanish flower whose flawless face rose to haunt him in every fevered dream. He would escape on a pirate ship bent on plunder—and then one day return as conqueror to destroy all Maria's resistance in the smoldering fire of his embrace....

From lush Caribbean estates to desperate battles at sea, all the way to the glittering English and Spanish courts, Maria and Gabriel would rage against the one truth their hearts could never deny...and which passion alone could set free....[5]

Did you notice the common theme suggested in the titles and the plots? And the cover art for each book (90 percent of them look like they have been produced by the same artist!) pictures the same prevailing theme. There is a man and a woman locked in a wild, passionate embrace. Each wears an expression of ecstasy, or the young, exceptionally attractive heroine mirrors hesitant resistance on her face.

There is a strict code for the successful romance novel. Recently one university offered a course entitled, "How to Write and Sell a Romance Novel." Here is how the course was promoted:

> Romance will comprise an estimated 40 percent of all fiction published this year. This voracious reader appetite for romance novels has created an opportunity for writers who have never published before to break into print as editors actively seek to fill this demand.
>
> There are rules. The success formula for this category is underscored with rigid editorial requirements. This practical, results-oriented seminar will zero in on such basic topics as:
> • The romance formula
> • Shortcuts to creating an outline that "works"
> • Setting
> • Hooking the reader
> • Plotting and subplotting
> • Love scenes
> • Main characters and secondary characters
> • Dialogue
> • Conflict
> • Creating happy endings.
> Special attention will be given to the all important aspect of marketability—how to sell what you've written.

The public library is as much a treasury of romantic literature as the local bookstore. While in my local library recently I asked the librarian to show me the romance novels. "Do you see those bookcases with the chairs in front of them?" she indicated with a grin. "The shelves hold scores of novels and the chairs are for the stream of ladies who come to look for new books." She told me that some "romance addicts" become very upset if they cannot find any new novels on the shelves.

Some of them take it upon themselves to storm the library's storage room to look for any new books which may have arrived. Romance addiction seems to be approaching epidemic proportions!

Look back over the description of your imaginary best-selling novel. What does it tell you about your own view of romance? The following paragraphs will further help you evaluate the sources and expressions of your romantic ideals.

Romantic Fantasies and Facts

Let's take a trip into your romantic past for a few minutes. Our daily lives are accompanied by many romantic dreams and fantasies that have been part of our private world since childhood. All boys and girls occasionally escape to their inner dream worlds in which they are either rescued by a magnificent hero or they become the heroes themselves. Romantic fantasy is a part of growing up.

What were your childhood romantic fantasies like? Think through the questions listed below and write your responses in the space provided. Then take turns sharing your childhood and adolescent fantasies with your spouse. It is often easier for women to talk about childish fantasies, since we men dislike sharing anything that would seem to weaken our manly images. But these early heroic and romantic daydreams helped to create our manly image and are a vital part of the development process.

From the ages of 6-12, can you remember...
Your favorite romantic comic strip characters? Fairy tales? Novels? Movies?

Who was the hero of your daydreams?

Who was the romantic object of your fantasies?

From the ages of 13-18, can you remember...
Your favorite romantic comic strip characters? Fairy tales? Novels? Movies?

Who was the hero of your daydreams?

Who was the romantic object of your fantasies?

Let's attempt to define romance again. Romance has been called an invisible energy that may or may not be mutual in a relationship between a man and a woman. The attraction of romance is a sense of excitement that one person experiences at the thought of, or in the presence of, another. It is a powerful desire to be with that person in an intimate way. And when romance strikes, it strikes without reason. Physical affection and sex may be included in the romantic relationship or they may not be present at all, since they are just two facets of romance.

Feelings of romance also create a desire to be special and valuable to, and well thought of by, the romantic object. There is a desire for belonging, companionship and intimacy. When the romantic attraction is high, you desire to be with that individual as much as possible. And you want the other person to have the same feelings about you. You want that special person to want you. Life is less pleasant when you are apart.

In a mutual attraction, there is a shared sense of delight and excitement in both partners. There is a feeling that something very special and even unusual is occurring between you. All of life is viewed through the filter of your romantic feelings and experiences.

The moment by moment delight of romance is enjoyed, but there is also a strong desire for permanency. "I want what we have to last forever," you say. In courting couples, there are concerns over losing each other or seeing romance wane. Prior to a marriage commitment, couples often pledge themselves to one another with statements like, "Our romance will never change. It will always be this way. We will never let anything happen to it."

Romantic individuals are concerned about displeasing their partners since one cannot be happy if the other is unhappy with him or her. With intense romance individuals experience a feeling of vulnerability to their partners. During the honeymoon stage of marriage couples are more easily hurt through interpersonal adjustments than at later stages of marriage. The intense desire of newlyweds to be with each other and share one another's world can make them overly sensitive to disappointments, slights, or anything that resembles rejection. The slightest sense of displeasure from a partner becomes overbearing. Being so vulnerable can cause one to overreact and misinterpret a partner's actions.[6]

In the Mood for Romance

Is romance related only to erotic or physical love? Perhaps our definitions of romance in the past have limited its potential. I believe romance in marriage can be constantly present, although its intensity varies. There are peak moments of great romantic intensity, such as in physical lovemaking. But there are major portions of time when romance is no more intense than a quiet conversation, a smile or a gentle touch.

Romanticism does not always imply a sensational setting or erotic physical activity. Sensational settings and erotic activities are wonderful, but we do not dwell there. Too many would-be romantics tend to focus on these peak experiences and forget the less intense, but equally valid, expressions of romance in day-to-day living.

Daily romance is built upon many qualities that each partner expresses to the other: meeting needs, tenderness, consideration, sensitivity, thoughtfulness, listening and learning to speak your partner's language so that deep, intimate communication occurs. We can put forth tremendous thought and energy into creating mountaintop roman-

---

Too many would-be romantics tend to focus on peak experiences and forget the less intense, but equally valid, expressions of romance in day-to-day living.

---

tic settings, moods and occasions, but none of these special events can substitute for words and actions of daily romance.

One couple described romance like this: "We could say that romance is a mental, emotional, and physical communion two people share, which may be enhanced by 'romantic' moods and settings and touches. But romance is not a setting. It is the relationship we have as soul-mates, which can be taken into and out of a wide variety of settings, 'romantic' ones included."[7]

I think of many romantic high points that my wife Joyce and I have experienced. Some of them just happened and others we helped happen.

A few years ago we were in Grand Teton National Park for our annual Marriage Enrichment Seminar. After the last evening meeting was over we got into our car to drive back to our cabin through the light snowfall. The radio was tuned to an a cappella men's choir singing a secular love song. We listened as we drove back and when we reached the cabin, instead of going inside, we just sat in the car for a couple of minutes, quietly listening to the words of the song and watching the gentle snow fall.

When it was over we went inside. Later that night we both commented, "Wasn't that a special time?"—and we agreed that it was. Perhaps it would not have been special to anyone else, but to us there was a sense of closeness and intimacy in being together at that moment. For us, that was romantic.

On other occasions we create a romantic atmosphere in our family room at home. For our twenty-fifth wedding anniversary, instead of spending money on a trip, we had our backyard landscaped to resemble a miniature mountain scene. We have a little (four foot) hill, a waterfall and a trickling stream which feeds a couple of pools. There is a small footbridge and pine, birch and liquid amber trees, which provide us with ample fall colors. Our mountain scene can be viewed from our family room through sliding glass doors.

Some evenings Joyce and I put one of our favorite John Denver albums on the stereo, turn out the lights and sit together on the couch holding hands, listening to the music of the record and the waterfall. The outdoor lights accent the waterfall and the trees. We may sit there for 30 or 40 minutes not saying much, but listening and enjoying and feeling very content and comfortable. It is a romantic time for us. There are other times of romance too, but I'm not going into detail on those!

What about your planned and unplanned romantic moments? Use the following exercise to evaluate the romance in your relationship.

Step One
1. What is romantic about your daily life together? Describe.

2. What actions on your part create romance for you? What actions on your spouse's part create romance for you?

3. Describe a romantic getaway you would like to experience with your spouse. Where would it be? What would you do? How would it be different from your daily life? What would you wear? Where would you eat? What would be the decor, music, fragrances, conversation topics, etc.?

4. What would it take for item 3 to actually happen?

5. How could you create at home what you just described in item 3?

Step Two

1. When we were dating, we created and sustained romance by...

2. When it comes to romance in our marriage now, my view is...
   a. Our life together is one sustained romantic "high."
   b. We are romantic, but at times I feel we are getting less and less romantic.
   c. We do have a romantic side of us that we can turn on when we want to.
   d. Maybe someday we will be able to be romantic.
   e. We're too old for romance.
   f. Who needs it? We are sensible and stable.
   g. We have more important things to do than get involved with romance.
   h. What's romance?

3. When it comes to romance...
    a. I am the romantic. You are practical and realistic.
    b. You are the romantic. I am practical and realistic.
    c. Both of us are romantic, but in our own way.
    d. Neither of us has a romantic bone in our body.

4. Sometimes I get romantic and you don't respond. When this happens I feel...

5. Sometimes you get romantic and I don't respond. When this happens I feel...

6. Sometimes I am unable to get romantic with you because...
    a. I am too critical of you.
    b. I feel you are critical of me.
    c. I hold too many resentments from the past.
    d. My mind is elsewhere, like on daily practical concerns.
    e. I'm concerned that you might reject me or not respond when I become romantic.
    f. I like to get romantic first because I am more of an initiator than a responder.

7. One way I would like us to be romantic at this point in our marriage is...[8]

What Makes a Romance?

A romantic relationship can have a number of important ingredients. First, romance often includes the element of the unexpected. The routines and tasks of our daily lives consume most of our time and energy. An unexpected romantic surprise can help break up the routine and monotony of the day. Surprises also carry the message, "I'm thinking about you. You're on my mind. I want your day to be different."

Presenting flowers or a gift for no special occasion or no special reason adds to the sense of romance. I enjoy creating surprises for my wife, Joyce. These range from the humorous to the serious. Since we enjoy eating out together, I will often search out a new restaurant that I think she will enjoy and take her there without telling her where we are going. I've even taken her on brief trips that were a total surprise to her. Sometimes she's opened a cupboard to find a banner I've placed there that says, "I love you."

You may have your own routine established for creating special romantic surprises. That's important. But beware: Anything that is repeated month after month, year after year, or decade after decade may become humdrum. Surprising your spouse with dinner out at the same restaurant every payday may not be as romantic after 20 years! Why not look for new restaurants, activities, and ways to say, "I love you," that keep the excitement of the unexpected in your romancing?

A second element in a romantic relationship is called dating—something you used to do and hopefully still do. Dating means selecting a specific time to be together and making plans for the event. Sometimes a couple may mutually plan the activity or one person may be appointed to plan the date.

Most of the time romantic dating is just for the two of you and not a crowd! And when you're out on a date, I would suggest not talking about work or the children. Rather, talk about yourselves. Make it a fun time. Laugh and enjoy each other and be a little crazy. When you go to a restaurant, let the host or hostess know that you and your spouse are there on a date.

Dates ought to center on an activity where you can interact together. If you attend a movie or play, plan time before or after the show to eat and talk together. (In a later chapter there will be many suggestions for creative things to do on dates.)

I have been impressed with some ministers who have made an announcement like the following from the pulpit: "If any of you ask my wife and I to attend a gathering on the first or third Friday of the month, we will thank you for the invitation, but we will have to decline. Those nights are our date nights together and we do not let anything interfere with those special evenings. And if any of you would like to know what we do on a date, you're free to ask!" An announcement like that may send some shock waves through the congregation. Couples in leadership, however, who make romance a priority, provide a healthy role model for all of the couples in the congregation.

Third, because romance is often emotional and nonrational, a

If your spouse can predict what you will say, how you will respond, what kind of gift you will give on special occasions, then you are in a romantic rut.

---

romantic relationship sometimes includes the impractical. You may splurge on an outing or a gift, which you know you can't really afford, but the romantic value makes it worth scrimping in other areas to pay for it. Or consider an out-of-the-ordinary event like inviting your spouse to a "famous" French restaurant in the countryside. Pack an inexpensive picnic dinner, take a tape recorder with some French songs and a picture book on France from the library to look through together.

Impractical romantic happenings are moments to remember. And that's what romance is so often built upon—good memories. Store your hearts with romantic memories and they will carry you through the difficult times.

A fourth element in a romantic relationship is creativity. The French picnic dinner is an example of creative romance. Discover what delights your partner and then make those delights happen in many different, creative ways. Even the way you express your love to your partner each day can be varied and innovative. If your spouse can predict what you will say, how you will respond, what kind of gift you will give on special occasions, then you are in a romantic rut.

I like what Joseph Dillow tells husbands about being creative lovers. He has developed the following lighthearted test to help husbands evaluate their creativity in romance:

> To find out just how creative you are as a husband, may I suggest you take the following "Lover's Quotient Test." Give yourself ten points for each item on the following list if you have done it once in the past six months. If you have done any item on the list two or more times you get 20 points.

- Have you phoned her during the week and asked her out for one evening that weekend without telling her where you are taking her? A mystery date.
- Have you given her an evening completely off? You clean up the kitchen; you put the kids to bed.
- Have you gone parking with her at some safe and secluded spot and kissed and talked for an evening?
- Have you drawn a bath for her after dinner? Put a scented candle in the bathroom, add bath oil to the bath, send her there right after dinner, and then you clean up and put the kids to bed while she relaxes. (My wife says in order to get any points for this you must also clean up the tub!)
- Have you phoned her from work to tell her you were thinking nice thoughts about her? (You get *no* points for this one if you asked what was in the mail.)
- Have you written her a love letter and sent it special delivery? (First class mail will do.)
- Have you made a tape recording of all the reasons you have for loving her? Give it to her wrapped in a sheer negligee!

- Have you given her a day off? You clean the house, fix the meals, and take care of the kids. (My wife says you ought to get 30 points for this!)
- Have you put a special effects stereo recording of ocean waves on tape and played it while you had a nude luau on the living room floor? (If this seems a little far out for your tastes, you could substitute by either removing the stereo effects tape or having a popcorn party in the privacy of the bedroom instead.)
- Have you spent a whole evening (more than two hours) sharing mutual goals and planning family objectives with her and the children?
- Have you ever planned a surprise weekend? You make the reservations and arrange for someone to keep the children for two days. Tell her to pack her suitcase, but don't tell her where you are going. (Just be sure it's *not* the Super Bowl!) Make it someplace romantic.
- Have you picked up your clothes just one time in the past six months and put them on hangers?
- Have you given her an all-over body massage with scented lotion and a vibrator?
- Have you spent a session of making love to her that included at least two hours of romantic conversation, shared dreams, many positions of intercourse, and much variety of approach and caresses?
- Have you repaired something around the house which she has *not* requested?
- Have you kissed her passionately for at least 30 seconds one morning just before you left for work, or one evening when you walked in the door?
- Have you brought her an unexpected little gift like perfume, a ring, or an item of clothing?
- Have you replaced her old negligee?

I have given this ridiculous test to men all over the country. Let's see how your score compares with theirs:

200-360—LOVER: You undoubtedly have one of the most satisfied wives in the country.

150-200—GOOD: Very few make this category.

100-150—AVERAGE: This husband is somewhat typical and usually not very exciting as a lover.

50-100—KLUTZ: Too many score in this category. I hope you'll begin to move up soon.

0-50—HUSBAND: There is a difference between a "husband" and a "lover." The only reason your wife is still married to you is that she's a Christian, she has unusual capacity for unconditional acceptance, and there are some verses in the Bible against divorce.

While the test shouldn't be taken too seriously, it does outline a plan of attack to increase your creativity level. I realize that many things on the list may not fit your temperament and your marriage relationship. *Make up your own list.* The idea is simply to encourage creativity in a fun way.[9]

Now you know what creativity is all about!

Fifth, romance involves daily acts of care, concern, love, speaking your partner's language, listening and giving each other your personal attention. Such acts convey a message of acceptance and thoughtfulness to your spouse. You see, romance begins in your mind and not in your glands. Too many people, especially men, tend to let their physical drives take the lead in romance all the time. Rather, a thoughtful, caring attitude will create romance even when your glands are stuck in neutral.

Sixth, romance involves commitment. Every day of our lives as couples is marked by highs and lows, joys and disappointments. Romantic feelings will ebb and flow. But if commitment to each other is at the heart of the marriage relationship, romance will thrive. Mutual commitment creates a mutual love response, and commitment is first an exercise of the will based on an attitude of heart. Here's how one husband described the process:

> Being an artist at romance does not require so much a sentimental and emotional nature as it requires a thoughtful nature. When we think of the romantic things, we think of events that occur because someone made a choice to love. A man stops off at a florist and brings his wife a single rose in the evening, a girl makes her lover a lemon pie with just the degree of tartness he likes, a wife makes arrangements for her husband to take the caribou-hunting trip he thought he'd never afford— these are not the goo of sweet emotion, they are the stuff that comes from resolution and determination, and they are strong mortar.[10]

Notes
1. *Webster's New Collegiate Dictionary* (Springfield, MA: G. & C. Merriam Company, Publishers, 1977), p. 996.
2. *Webster's New Collegiate Dictionary*, p. 996.
3. Alan Loy McGinnis, *The Romance Factor* (San Francisco: Harper and Row, Publishers, Inc., 1982), p. 38.
4. Cassie Edwards, *Savage Heart* (New York: Zebra Books, 1985), back cover.
5. Shirlee Busbee, *Spanish Rose* (New York: Avon Books, 1986), back cover.
6. Harold Bessell, *The Love Test* (New York: William Morrow Company, 1984), adapted from pp. 35-36.
7. Ed and Candee Neuenschwander, *Two Friends in Love: Growing Together in Marriage* (Portland, OR: Multnomah Press, 1986), p. 44. Used by permission.
8. David Luecke, *The Relationship Manual* (Columbia, MD: The Relationship Institute, 1981), adapted from p. 74.
9. Reprinted by permission of Thomas Nelson Publishers from the book *SOLOMON ON SEX*, Copyright © 1977 by Joseph Dillow.
10. McGinnis, *The Romance Factor*, p. 198.

THREE

No Intimacy? No Romance!

*H*ow do you feel about intimacy?" I asked several men and women that question and their responses were interesting. Here are some of them:

"Oh, intimacy is wonderful!"

"You've got to have it. You can't have a relationship without it."

"What's intimacy? I don't know what you're talking about."

"Oh, I'm all for sex. It's a must."

"I guess it's all right with the right person."

"Intimacy? I guess I've never thought too much about it. Well, I guess my partner and I are intimate. I'll ask her."

Intimacy is a widely used word. People talk about being intimate with one another. But too often the word is misunderstood and misused. Intimacy is an essential ingredient for continuing romance and deep relationships. In fact, I will be so bold as to say: *For true love and romance to exist in a relationship, intimacy must be present!* Is that strong enough?

Since there is so much confusion over intimacy, perhaps we need to define it. The word intimacy is derived from the Latin word *intimus* meaning "inmost." Intimacy suggests a very strong personal relationship, a special *emotional* closeness that includes understanding and being understood by someone who is very special. Intimacy has also been defined as "an affectionate bond, the strands of which are composed of mutual caring, responsibility, trust, open communication of feelings and sensations, as well as the non-defended interchange of

---

The closeness of intimacy involves private and personal interaction, commitment and caring.

---

information about significant emotional events."[1] Intimacy means taking the risk to be close to someone and allowing that someone to step inside your personal boundaries.

Sometimes intimacy can hurt. As you lower your defenses to let each other close, you reveal the real, intimate, secret you to each other, including your weaknesses and faults. With the real you exposed, you become vulnerable to possible ridicule from your partner. The risk of pain is there, but the rewards of intimacy greatly overshadow the risk. As one writer states:

> It is not intimacy itself, therefore, which is so distasteful and intimidating to the world, but rather the moral condemnation that comes with it. People crave closeness with one another, but are repelled by the sin that such closeness inevitably uncovers in themselves: the selfish motives that are unmasked, the pettiness that spills out, the monstrous new image of self that emerges as it struggles so pitifully to have its own way.[2]

Intimacy means vulnerability but it also means security. The openness can be scary, but the acceptance each partner offers in the midst of vulnerability provides a wonderful sense of security. Intimate couples can feel safe and accepted—fully exposed perhaps, yet fully accepted.

Intimacy can occur outside of a marriage commitment and without the element of physical love. Women can be intimate with women and men with men. The closeness of intimacy involves private and personal interaction, commitment and caring. We can speak of intimacy between friends as well as intimacy between spouses.

Intimacy can exist without marriage, but it is impossible for a meaningful marriage to exist without intimacy. For two hearts to touch each other, intimacy is a must. If you don't know how your partner thinks and feels about various issues or concerns, that individual is somewhat of a stranger to you. And for two hearts to be bonded together, the strangers must leave.

It is often assumed that intimacy automatically occurs between married partners. But I've seen far too many "strangers" get married. I've talked to too many husbands and wives who feel isolated from each other and lonely even after many years of marriage. I've heard statements like: "We share the same house, the same table and the same bed, but we might as well be strangers"; "We've lived together for 23 years and yet I don't know my spouse any better now than when we married"; "What really hurts is that we can spend a weekend together and I still feel lonely. I think I married someone who would have preferred being a hermit in some ways." No, intimacy is not automatic. Communication is the vehicle for creating and maintaining intimacy. Communication is the means by which we know another person.

Are We Intimate?

Take a moment to evaluate the intimacy in your marriage relationship. Explore how you deal with intimacy as a couple by circling your response to the following statements. Work through the exercise separately, then explain your responses to each other:

1. When it comes to conversational intimacy, the way I see our relationship is...

    a. We say a lot but reveal little of our real selves.
    b. We reveal our real selves but we don't say very much.
    c. We say a lot and reveal a lot of our real selves.
    d. We say little and reveal little of our real selves.

2. When it comes to sharing with you what I am really thinking, feeling, wanting, or not wanting...

    a. I keep my inner-self well hidden.
    b. I reveal as much as I feel safe to share.
    c. I let it all hang out.

3. When it comes to sharing with me what you are really thinking, feeling, wanting, or not wanting...

    a. You seem to keep your inner-self well hidden.
    b. You seem to reveal as much as you feel safe to share.
    c. You seem to let it all hang out.

4. Some ways I avoid intimacy when we are getting uncomfortably close are...

    a. I laugh or crack a joke.
    b. I shrug it off and act as if it doesn't matter.
    c. I act confused—like I don't know what is going on.
    d. I look angry so that you can't see into me too deeply.
    e. I get angry or huffy, especially when I am feeling vulnerable.
    f. I get overly talkative.
    g. I get analytical—hiding behind a wall of intellectualizing.
    h. I change the subject so I won't have to deal with it.
    i. I act strong, together, above-it-all—especially when feeling vulnerable.

5. From the list above, some ways I see you avoid intimacy when we are getting uncomfortably close are...

6. The reason I avoid intimacy this way is...

7. The effect of avoiding intimacy in this way is...

8. In order to build intimacy in our relationship, I would now be willing to...[3]

Intimate Conversations

There are five levels of conversation corresponding to degrees of intimacy in a marriage relationship. As you read about each level, pause to complete the "Evaluate" section as it relates to your marriage.

The first level of conversation is limited to sharing facts, explanations or information. Conversations at this level are much like exchanging newspaper stories. While the information can be interesting, it is often considered small talk and really does not accomplish much in getting to know another person. The degree of intimacy at this conversation level is extremely shallow.

Evaluate
1. When does this type of conversation occur in your marriage?

2. Which of you tends to use this style of conversation most?

3. What percentage of your conversation tends to occur at this level?

10% 20% 30% 40% 50% 60% 70% 80% Oops—trouble!

The second level of conversation centers on sharing the ideas and opinions of other people. Conversation at this level is a bit more interesting and yet discloses very little of oneself. Practically no intimacy is achieved when discussion is limited to persons outside the relationship.

Evaluate
1. When does this type of conversation occur in your marriage?

2. Which of you tends to use this style of conversation most?

3. What percentage of your conversation tends to occur at this level?

10% 20% 30% 40% 50% 60% 70% 80% Still trouble!

Conversation level three produces moderate intimacy. At this level you are sharing your own ideas and opinions. You are disclosing some of your own thoughts and risking minor vulnerability, but you are still not revealing who you really are.

Evaluate
1. When does this type of conversation occur in your marriage?

2. Which of you tends to use this style of conversation most?

3. What percentage of your conversation tends to occur at this level?

    10% 20% 30% 40% 50% 60% 70% 80% Getting better!

4. Name two people you share with on this level.

Level four involves a higher degree of intimacy in conversation. Now you are sharing personal preferences, beliefs, concerns, and also some of your own personal experiences. One of the level four questions my daughter often asked me when she was young was, "Daddy, what were you like when you were a little boy?" I was amazed at how much I would begin to recall and share about myself in response to her question.

Evaluate
1. When does this type of conversation occur in your marriage?

2. Which of you tends to use this style of conversation most?

3. What percentage of your conversation tends to occur at this level?

    10% 20% 30% 40% 50% 60% 70% 80% Quite good!

4. Name two people you share with on this level.

Level five is the highest level of conversation and communication. Here you share your inner feelings and preferences, likes and dislikes.

You share what is occurring within your inner life and you open up completely. You move beyond talking about events or beliefs or ideas or opinions to talking about how these ideas or events or people influence you and how they touch you emotionally and inwardly. At this level, emotional expression has moved from talking from the head to talking from the heart.

Evaluate

1. When does this type of conversation occur in your marriage?

2. Which of you tends to use this style of conversation most?

3. What percentage of your conversation tends to occur at this level?

   10% 20% 30% 40% 50% 60% 70% 80% Magnificent!

4. Name two people you share with on this level.

   Let's go a bit deeper. You and your partner each take a sheet of paper and complete the exercise below. Do not discuss your responses until you are both finished.

1. I see myself as being emotionally open in the following manner:
   a. I throw open the door and let it all hang out.
   b. I open the door, but tend to keep my hand on the doorknob just in case.
   c. I open the door halfway to see what happens.
   d. I open the door a crack and peek out.

    e. I use deadbolt locks and barricade the door.
    f. Where's the door?

2. I see you as being emotionally open in the following manner:
    a. You throw open the door and let it all hang out.
    b. You open the door, but tend to keep your hand on the door-knob just in case.
    c. You open the door halfway to see what happens.
    d. You open the door a crack and peek out.
    e. You use deadbolt locks and barricade the door.
    f. Do you know where the door is?

3. The emotions I have difficulty expressing openly are...
    a. fear
    b. disappointment
    c. pleasure
    d. sadness
    e. resentment
    f. hurt
    g. frustration
    h. anxiety
    i. anger
    j. joy
    k. delight
    l. elation
    m. love

4. What do you do when you have difficulty expressing one of these emotions?

5. What does your spouse do when he/she has difficulty expressing one of these emotions?

6. Which emotion is the easiest for you to express? Which is the easiest for your spouse to express?

For emotional intimacy to occur in this exercise, the next step is vital. Sit face-to-face with your partner (which also means knee-to-knee) and hold hands. Holding hands increases the intimacy and also tends to keep a lid on any temptation to get upset. Take turns sharing your responses with one another. You might even begin by asking your spouse how he/she feels about responding to the questions and discussing them in this manner. Be sure you conclude your time by discussing what you can do to increase the level of emotional conversation in your relationship.

(NOTE: There are several books that can provide additional help in the area of intimacy. For men I recommend *The Secrets Men Keep* (Doubleday and Co.), by Ken Druck and *The McGill Report on Male Intimacy* (Harper and Row), by Michael McGill. Both of these are exceptional resources. For women I suggest my book, *Understanding the Man in Your Life* (Word Books).

Sharing Your Feelings

As you move deeper into the world of intimacy, you must learn to listen to your own feelings. They will tell you how you are experiencing life. Share with your spouse both your good and bad feelings. Your spouse cannot know you unless you invite him or her into your inner world. Verbalizing feelings greatly minimizes guessing, misunderstanding and arguing, and creates greater empathy and support between partners.

Listen to your spouse without judgment. Listen to his/her words and nonverbal messages. Try to determine if the feelings behind the words are good or bad. Many people feel free to share positive feelings or what they think others want to hear. But baring personal flaws, hurts

---

When we can trust our feelings, and then in turn trust them to others, we build strong bonds of intimacy.

---

and less acceptable emotions is painful and frustrating. Learn to share and hear both good and bad feelings.

I don't know how many times in counseling I have heard the statement from a husband or wife, "I've been hurting inside for years and now there is nothing left of my love." The long-standing hurt may be real, but the individual was unfair to his or her partner for not communicating these feelings and building intimacy through the years. No one is a mind reader! How can your spouse possibly know about your inner hurts and disappointments unless you talk about them?

I like the definition of emotions I read recently:

> Our emotions are the movements of our soul. They are the sensations we experience that bear the labels of joy, grief, pain, disillusionment, love, delight, warmth, astonishment, fright. They are the stirrings of our inner persons reflected in our cellular shells. Also, emotions are the subterranean shifts in feeling we encounter that aren't necessarily activated by sight, hearing, taste, or smell—though they may be. These inside movements, stirrings, or sensations may change several times an hour. They

may occur in multiples, forming duets and trios that sometimes produce harmony and at other times create dissonance.[4]

There are many people today who honestly do not know how to express their emotions. They have been raised emotionally sheltered or inhibited in some ways. They have lost the distinction between thinking and feeling. Or they find excuses to avoid the deeper levels of conversation where emotions are verbalized.

But consider this: There is no aphrodisiac in the world as strong and powerful as an ongoing, deep level of communication that flows from one person to another. Sexual intimacy and fulfillment spring from conversational intimacy. There are no shortcuts or techniques that can substitute for honest expression of inner feelings.

Yes, intimacy involves time and energy and the willingness to be a risk-taker. I have heard scores of excuses for avoiding conversational intimacy, most often based on a lack of time or energy. Most excuses can be summed up as fear and lack of desire. We have to make time and take time! We find time for our work, television programs, sports, hobbies and other activities and relationships. Why not take time for marital intimacy?

The Benefits of Openness

Men and women need to stop viewing feelings as enemies and start seeing them as allies. Consider the benefits to acknowledging and expressing our feelings.

Feelings motivate people. They challenge us to do our best and assist us in some of our greatest accomplishments. Tapping into feelings is a tremendous energy source.

Feelings create a healthy environment. Ignoring feelings depletes energy, whereas by expressing them the air is cleared and we move on in life. We do not become stuck with excess baggage from the past. Expressing feelings is one of the best ways of reducing stress.

Feelings are the bridge to other people. When we can trust our feelings, and then in turn trust them to others, we build strong bonds of intimacy. Relating to others on the level of feelings means that we relate *with* them rather than *at* them.

When we express our feelings, we build self-confidence. We tend to believe more in who we are and what we can do. We no longer have to live in fear of others discovering our feelings.

Feelings help us make the correct decisions. Those who are in close touch with their feelings are more prepared to make difficult decisions and take important actions than those who are not.

Feelings help to heal both old and new wounds. If you are hurt, you don't have to stay hurt. Feelings help us forgive others and also complete unfinished business.

Feelings give us life, since they are an endless source of fresh new energy. They bring beauty into our souls.

Feelings and their expression give us another language with which to communicate with people and with God.[5]

If you really want to build intimacy in your marriage you will need to take three steps. First, identify and eliminate the hindrances to intimacy that many couples experience. This means you can no longer claim the excuses of no time or no energy.

Second, evaluate your present level of marital intimacy. Be sure to talk through all the exercises in this chapter together. Use the following chart to discuss nine specific areas of intimacy in your marriage.

Third, involve yourselves in the following exercise. Spend an entire day together as a couple. Easy? Maybe not in the way I am about to suggest. Commit yourselves to remain in the same room alone together for at least 12 hours. "Alone" means no other people, no books, no television, radio or stereo, and no telephone calls. If you have children, be sure they are taken care of by others so no distractions of any kind will occur.

Be sure you have a bathroom adjacent to the room you choose and have a good supply of your favorite foods and beverages on hand. If your home does not guarantee the privacy you need, check into a motel room or cabin for a day. Your agreement must be to stay togeth-

MARITAL INTIMACY CHECKUP[6]
(Instructions: After discussing each area, check the blanks
that apply to your relationship.)

Facts of Intimacy	Both Desire Improvement	Wife Desires Improvement	Husband Desires Improvement	Both Satisfied
1. Sexual Intimacy				
2. Emotional Intimacy (Being tuned to each other's wavelength)				
3. Intellectual Intimacy (Closeness in the world of ideas)				
4. Aesthetic Intimacy (Sharing in acts of creating beauty)				
5. Creative Intimacy (Sharing in acts of creating together)				
6. Recreational Intimacy (Relating in experiences of fun and play)				
7. Work Intimacy (Closeness of sharing common tasks)				
8. Crisis Intimacy (Closeness in coping with problems and pain)				
9. Conflict Intimacy (Facing and struggling with differences)				

er in the room for 12 hours no matter what, even if you sit in silence for a few minutes or hours. You may feel awkward, uneasy or self-conscious. You may even begin to think of ways to break the commitment. But determine to stick it out for the full period.

In time you will begin to talk. You may talk about anything as long as it is personal. Do not talk about items like the house, the children or work. Talk about yourselves and your relationship. If either of you slips and brings up a nonpersonal topic, you must share a feeling about what you brought up and then move back to talking about your own relationship.

Most couples experience a deepening of feelings as the hours pass and they begin to share in a way they have not experienced before. Some couples pray together, sing together, make love or enjoy any combination of many intimate expressions. Many have made the 12-hour retreat a biannual or annual event in order to continue developing intimacy in their relationship.

Comparing the Sexes

Some of you reading this chapter may desperately want your spouse to become more intimately responsive. And some of you may wish you or your spouse had never read this chapter. Becoming intimate in this manner can be threatening both to the person who has never revealed much before and to a partner who has not heard much from his/her spouse before. You may feel overwhelmed or you may not know how to respond in the most appropriate manner. Yes, there is a risk to intimacy, but the potential benefits outweigh the risks.

Is it easier for men or women to develop the style of intimacy suggested here? Some people from both sexes simply are more skilled in expressing their feelings. Some people speak the language of feelings easily and others must learn it with difficulty. But generally speaking, women are more apt to express their inner selves and feelings than men. Ken Druck has described the approach that we men take toward intimacy:

Men today are the guardians of some of the world's best-kept secrets. We lead secret emotional lives, often hiding our deepest fears and insecurities, as well as our most cherished dreams, even from those we love and trust. Perhaps we are hiding a fear we have carried around our entire life, perhaps a secret fantasy. Or we may be more sensitive and, as a consequence, more easily hurt than we care to admit.

We block off entire areas of ourselves, stamp them "TOP SECRET," and file them away. And we keep their existence a secret from wives, girlfriends, children and buddies. We see these parts of who we are as a threat. Perhaps they embarrass us. Or maybe they fail to confirm a particular image we have set out to project for others....

We select any number of places in which to hide our secrets. We disguise them in roles like "Mr. Nice Guy" or "The Hard-driving Businessman." Our former jobs and failed marriages may have been burial grounds for secrets. Even our greatest successes can become hiding places for our deepest secrets.

But secrets have a way of making their presence felt. We may think that we are done with them, having filed them away and forgotten about them. But they are still there, often disguised in a stubborn feeling of unhappiness or uneasiness that refuses to go away.[7]

Men, for whatever reason, we may need to work harder than our wives at developing the emotional transparency that leads to intimacy and romance in our marriages.

The Priority of Prayer

Earlier I suggested that conversational intimacy is the basis for physical intimacy between married partners. Let's take intimacy a step further. For conversational intimacy to develop to its fullest, the level of intimacy between you and your heavenly Father provides an important foundation. Remember the five levels of conversation identified earlier in this chapter? Consider your own personal prayer life and relationship to Jesus Christ in light of these five levels. As the level of communication deepens between you and God, you will begin to experience a greater strength and courage to deepen the levels between you and your partner. God's plans for your marriage are best fulfilled when each

> *As the level of communication deepens between you and God, you will begin to experience a greater strength and courage to deepen the levels between you and your partner.*

of you are open to His presence and guidance. Prayer, then, is the first step toward marital intimacy.

The next step, even before you venture into conversational intimacy, is sharing yourself with your spouse in prayer together. The majority of Christian couples do not exercise this special element in their relationships. I'm sure there are many reasons why Christian partners do not pray together. Perhaps you know some of those reasons from your own hesitance to pray with your spouse.

Often one partner wants to pray but the other is hesitant. Perhaps one is not accustomed to praying out loud and, in comparing himself/herself to his/her partner, feels very inadequate. Or one partner has never developed a personal prayer life and communicating with God is foreign to him/her. Couples may feel that they must pray together every day for at least 15 to 20 minutes. But because of the hectic pace of their lives, a couple finds a prayer schedule difficult to achieve, so nothing happens.

How many of us have ever been taught how to pray together as couples? Very few, I suspect. How many of us have any prayer models—couples who pray together regularly and are willing to share with us what they have learned and how prayer has drawn them closer together in their relationship? Again, I don't see many hands raised. For most of us, developing an intimate prayer relationship with our spouses is an assignment we accept with very little training or example.

Praying together is a time of coming together in the presence of God. There is no "right" amount of time to spend praying. Often couples begin by taking a minute or two to share concerns and requests. Then they pray silently together. After establishing this practice they may feel more comfortable praying aloud together. Some couples take a brief time after a date to share and pray. They pray for each other at specific times during the day as well. Other couples pray at the evening meal. Some couples read a book together on the subject of prayer or, as Joyce and I have done, read aloud from a daily devotional resource such as my book, *Quiet Times for Couples* (Harvest House).

It is when you pray together that communication barriers are broken, wills are made more pliable, and your heart reaches out to your spouse. The honesty of praying together out loud to God in the presence of your partner frees you to continue that honest communication as you look into the eyes of your spouse.

The Holy Spirit can minister to you and your marriage when, through prayer, you give Him access to your lives. Intimacy begins with God and you alone, then as a couple together in His presence, and finally touching one another's lives with the gifts of your emotions and trust. And there is a safeguard that protects us as we open ourselves to another person. That safeguard is God's love.

> And so it is in marriage that when the Lord draws a man and a woman together in the most intimate of human associations, He does so by giving them His love, which is the only thing that can shield them through the searing experience of self-revelation they are to undergo. This is an experience that all peo-

ple both crave and fear, with a fear that is conquerable only by love. Only love can drive out the constant threat of condemnation and rejection that otherwise haunts and spoils all experiences of intimacy.[8]

Notes

1. Source unknown.
2. From the book *The Mystery of Marriage* by Mike Mason, copyright 1985 by Multnomah Press, Portland, Oregon 97266, p. 84. Used by permission.
3. David L. Leucke, *The Relationship Manual* (Columbia, MD: The Relationship Institute, 1981), adapted from p. 25.
4. Ed and Candee Neuenschwander, *Two Friends in Love: Growing Together in Marriage* (Portland, OR: Multnomah Press, 1986), p. 135.
5. Excerpts from THE SECRETS MEN KEEP by Ken Druck, Ph.D., with James C. Simmons. Copyright © 1985 by Ken Druck, Ph.D. with James C. Simmons. Reprinted by permission of Doubleday and Company, Inc., adapted from pp. 35-36.
6. Howard J. Clinebell, Jr. and Charlotte H. Clinebell, *The Intimate Marriage* (San Francisco: Harper and Row, Publishers, Inc., 1970), pp. 37-38.
7. Druck, *The Secrets Men Keep*, p. 13. Used by permission.
8. Mason, *The Mystery of Marriage*, p. 85. Used by permission.

~FOUR~

Love?
What Is It?

*D*o *you know the difference between love and infatuation? I* can imagine a high school girl making the distinction, "Infatuation is thinking your boyfriend is as handsome as Kevin Costner, as intellectual as Albert Einstein, as amusing as Rodney Dangerfield, as devout as Billy Graham and as athletic as Hulk Hogan. But love is realizing that your guy is as handsome as Albert Einstein, as intellectual as Hulk Hogan, as amusing as Billy Graham, as devout as Kevin Costner, and as athletic as Rodney Dangerfield—but sticking with him anyway!"

Infatuation basically means infected with folly. A person is infatuated when he or she is inspired with a foolish or extravagant admiration for another person. Infatuation is a fantasy type of love. But the individual who is infatuated is convinced that it is real love since the pleasurable feelings associated with infatuation are often intense and overwhelming. But this type of "love" can fade rapidly simply through the process of getting to know one's heartthrob better.[1]

Love is more difficult to define. Some languages have multiple words for just one concept. The Swedish people, for example, have 53 words that convey the idea of cold. In the English speaking world, however, we tend to dissolve and condense a complex set of attitudes and emotions into a single word. The word "love" is a prime example. We toss the word around so much that it begins to take on numerous meanings. You may love football, love your pet alligator or love another person. Love can be defined as an attraction, desire, affection, delight, or admiration. It can also mean warm attachment, enthusiasm or devotion. Love may include the tenderness and sexual desire expressed by lovers. And to some people love means absolutely nothing—a score of zero in a tennis match!

What is your definition of married love? Before reading on, write down your own definition of the type of love you feel is necessary for a meaningful marriage relationship. Then write down what you think your spouse's definition would be. Ask your partner to complete the same exercise. After both of you have finished, discuss your responses.

My definition of love is:

My spouse's definition of love is:

Is It True Love?

myths of love

Let's consider a few facts about love: *No love at first sight*

1. Love at first sight is rare. An infatuated attraction may happen immediately but true love usually needs time to develop.

2. Love is NOT consistent. Your emotional response to your spouse will vary over the months, years and decades of a relationship.

3. Most individuals can fall in love many times. But the often involuntary physical and emotional attraction of "falling in love" should not be confused with the willful and abiding commitment to love selflessly the person who has captured your heart. *Not just once*

4. The quality of courtship love will change and deepen in marriage.
Love is not changeless

And each succeeding level of love can be as exciting, rewarding and fulfilling as the last.

5. *Love in a marriage relationship can diminish and even die.* Love must be carefully nurtured and cherished over the years if it is to endure the stress of two imperfect people living together.

6. *There is not just one person with whom an individual can be happily married.* "But," you may ask, "is there only one person selected by God for me to marry?" If you are certain that it is God's will for you to marry a particular person, then your question is answered and God validates it. And once you have married your chosen love, the "happily" part is mostly up to the two of you. As John Graham said, "Even if marriages are made in heaven, man has to be responsible for the maintenance."[2]

I also like what Scott Peck says in his book, *The Road Less Traveled,* about the illusion that erodes so many marriages today:

> To serve effectively as it does to trap us into marriage, the experience of falling in love probably must have as one of its characteristics the illusion that the experience will last forever....The myth of romantic love tells us, in effect, that for every young man in the world there is a young woman who was "meant for him," and vice versa. Moreover, the myth implies that there is only one man meant for a woman and only one woman for a man and this has been predetermined "in the stars." When we meet the person for whom we are intended, recognition comes through the fact that we fall in love. We have met the person for whom all the heavens intended us, and since the match is perfect, we will then be able to satisfy all of each other's needs forever and ever, and therefore live happily ever after in perfect union and harmony. Should it come to pass, however, that we do not satisfy or meet all of each other's needs and friction arises and we fall out of love, then it is clear that a dreadful mistake was made, we misread the stars, we did not hook up with our one and only perfect match, what we thought was love was

not real or "true" love, and nothing can be done about the situation except to love unhappily ever after or get divorced.[3]

Love is not something that just happens; it must be cultivated so it can grow. As I work with couples in premarital counseling, one of my goals is to discover the quality of love that they have for one another. If it is too idealistic or has a shallow base, I try to bring a sense of reality into their relationship. There are occasions when they do not want to hear the questions I ask. Sometimes they wonder why I do not accept their cliché-type answers, which do not always have the sense of realism that is needed.

I *want* the couples to experience some upset during the process of premarital counseling and to face some serious questions about one another and their future half century together. I want to eliminate as much as possible the unwanted, hurtful surprises of marriage so they can experience the fulfillment of some of their dreams. If they are truly in love, the questioning process doesn't diminish their love. Rather their love is strengthened and hopefully raised to a new level. If their love diminishes during this process, chances are there wasn't a sufficient foundation of love upon which to build a marriage.

I wonder how you would respond to some of the questions and assignments these couples complete during premarital counseling. If you and your spouse had come to me before you were married, how would you have answered these questions?

1. Describe the love that you have for your fiancé at this time in your life.

2. In light of what is happening to so many marriages today, why will yours succeed where so many others have failed? Why will yours be different? (And if the couple responds by saying, "Ours will succeed because we're Christians," I mention that most of my clients with marital difficulties or who divorce felt the same way when they married! Unfortunately, being a Christian is no guarantee of success. I persist by asking them what else will make the difference.)

3. What are 10 specific indications that this is the time of your life to marry?

4. What are 12 specific reasons why you want to marry the other person?

5. What are 25 expectations you have for your fiancé after you are married?

6. What are five specific needs your fiancé has in each of the following areas and how will he or she want these needs fulfilled after you are married: physical, emotional, intellectual, spiritual, social?

These are just a few of the questions I ask engaged couples. All of them are tied into the love response! Why do we push couples to deal with these realities? Perhaps Leo Buscaglia has the best answer:

> Learning to live with and love others requires skills as delicate as those of the surgeon, the master builder and the gourmet cook, none of whom would dream of practicing each profession without first acquiring the necessary knowledge. Still, we fragile, ill-equipped humans plow ahead, forming friendships, marrying, raising families with few or no actual resources at hand to meet the overwhelming demands. It is no surprise, therefore, that relationships which often begin with joyous wide-eyed naiveté too often end in disillusionment, bitterness and despair.[4]

Love Styles

People love and express their love in various ways. Let's consider six basic styles by which lovers carry on their relationships.

The *Best Friends* love style is a comfortable intimacy that develops over a period of time. Two individuals have a close association and share mutual interests together. Their love grows through companionship, rapport, mutual sharing and dependency and, over a period of time, self-revelation. It is rare at the beginning of the relationship for either person to believe that their friendship will develop into love or marriage.

The love that does develop and is expressed is more of a thoughtful, warm response and not so much romantic or passionate. Intensity of feeling is a bit foreign to this relationship. Intense arguments or displays of emotion are lacking. When there is a difference of opinion, rational discussions prevail since the couple can draw upon a depth of warm and mutual affection. They do not get upset when an argument occurs since conflict is no threat to their style of love. This type of love usually reflects stable and reasonable emotional responses. Commitment is very strong with this style of love.

A second style of love has been called *Game-playing Love.* To the game-playing lover, an emotional relationship is a contest to be won. Even when married these people seek a challenge to add spice to the relationship. Some even create risks to keep the marriage from becoming boring. Fighting and flirting are common. They do not like having demands placed upon them and they make few demands upon their partners. Unfortunately, they do tend to exploit their partners' feelings. *Game-playing Love* is a self-centered type of love relationship.

Logical Love is a style in which a person concentrates upon the practical values that can be found in the relationship. These people are very pragmatic and often have a list of what they are looking for in a mate. Romance does have some place in the relationship, but love to the logical lover should be an outgrowth of a couple's practical compatibility. Their love is stable as long as they perceive the relationship to be one of a fair exchange. Often these persons are quite selective before they settle upon the right person for a life-long partner. They are planners and they view life from this perspective.

The most unfulfilling and limiting type of love is *Possessive Love.* The possessive lover has a frantic need to know that he or she is loved. These people have frequent and intense emotional swings from elation to despair, from devotion to jealousy, and have a driving need to possess and be possessed by their partner. They are constantly searching for reassurance and are usually both dependent and demanding upon their partners. They are often passionate and they desire intense togetherness. Jealousy is seen as a part of love and if the person isn't jealous at some time, he may wonder if he is really in love.

In ancient times it was believed that this type of person was cursed by the gods, being a victim of some sort of divine madness. Such possessiveness is not madness; it is more likely emotional insecurity.

Romantic Love is best described as two people involved in a totally emotional relationship. Romantic lovers, whose symbol is Cupid's arrow

---

When couples become sensitive to each other's needs and discuss these differences openly, adjustments are made and each partner achieves satisfaction.

---

piercing a heart, are in love with love itself. Valentine's Day is as important to them as Christmas. Love at first sight is a necessity and a constant series of emotional highs are expected in the relationship. Physical attraction is very important, as are small and frequent romantic niceties and gestures. The romantic does not demand love from the other person, but is ready to lunge for it when it appears on the horizon.

To be a romantic, you must be willing to reveal yourself completely and to run the risk of emotional highs and lows. With such intensity bringing a couple together into marriage, the natural tapering off period of romance can be quite upsetting. The cool-down can either lead to substituting romantic fantasies for the sometimes unromantic real world or accepting a spouse's imperfections and working at rekindling the excitement. And many are able to do this.

Unselfish Love is a giving, forgiving, unconditionally caring and nurturing love. Self-sacrifice is involved. We love our partner even when he/she creates emotional pain for us. We respond more to the needs of our partner than to our own needs. Remember the Dickens classic, *A Tale of Two Cities*, in which one man goes to the guillotine in place of another? Both men loved the same woman, but Sydney Carton knew that Lucie Manette loved Charles Darnay more than she loved him. And for the sake of her happiness, Carton unselfishly gave up his own life. "It was a far, far better thing...than I have ever done," he said. *Unselfish Love* is expressed more perfectly in giving than in receiving.[5]

These then are the six styles of love. Do men tend more toward some styles and women toward others? What do you think? Let's look at them again. Decide which styles are more typical of men, which are more typical of women and which are equally represented by both sexes. Mark the chart below with your choices.

Typical of:	Men	Women	Both
Best Friend Love	☐	☑	☐
Game-playing Love	☑	☐	☐
Logical Love	☑	☐	☐
Possessive Love	☐	☐	☑
Romantic Love	☐	☑	☐
Unselfish Love	☐	☐	☑

Now if you have looked past the list to discover the answers, they are not here. How awful! You'll find them a little later, but first let's discuss another aspect of the subject.

What is your basic style of love, as determined from the brief descriptions above? Use the chart below to rate yourself on a scale of 0-10 for each style (0 means non-existent, 5 means average and 10 means very strong). Then do the same for your partner. When both of you have completed the exercise, share your responses with each other. Be sure to tell why you made the selections you did for yourself and your spouse. Spend time talking about those styles you would like to develop in yourself and those you would like to see develop in your spouse. Discuss how future development might occur.

You may discover that you are a combination of two or more styles. This is very common. Can you think of a combination of two that would be ideal? A suggested list will be given later.

Best Friend Love	1	2	3	4	5	6	7	8	9	10
Game-playing Love	1	2	3	4	5	6	7	8	9	10
Logical Love	1	2	3	4	5	6	7	8	9	10
Possessive Love	1	2	3	4	5	6	7	8	9	10
Romantic Love	1	2	3	4	5	6	7	8	9	10
Unselfish Love	1	2	3	4	5	6	7	8	9	10

Are there any best and worst combinations of styles between partners? So far there is very little research to indicate that partners with similar love styles are more apt to have more stable relationships than couples with differing styles. The key factor is whether we take our differences and adjust them to complement each other. Two individuals who have the same style can have a fulfilling relationship since they understand each other and are likely to reinforce each other. And two differing styles can be fulfilling if the couple learns to mesh emotionally with each other.

However, sameness in style can become a problem by producing either emotional destructiveness or boredom. And different styles can produce pain and frustration.[6]

When styles are intensely divergent, conflict and difficulties are more likely to occur. Not understanding the differing need levels for privacy and closeness is very common. Recognizing the differences and accepting them lessens the problems. But when couples become sensitive to each other's needs and discuss these differences openly, adjustments are made and each partner achieves satisfaction.

There are certain combinations of love styles that tend to bring greater harmony in relationships. (But remember: it is highly unlikely that a person possesses only one love style.) For example, two *Best Friend* types who marry can produce a lasting and loving relationship. On the other hand, two *Game-player* types may have a risky relationship because of their tendency to change.

A *Possessive* matched with a *Game-player* will also experience difficulty, as will a *Romantic* and a *Game-player.* I have found many cou-

---

Jesus Christ can fill the needs and lacks in our lives and free us to love in a biblical way.

---

ples where one is a *Romantic* and the other is a *Logical,* and as the years go by each becomes more entrenched in his/her own style. The more each tries to give his/her style of love to a partner of another style, the more they miss meeting the needs of that person. And a greater frustration is the result. In time many of them divorce.

But let me offer an opinion here. *I do not believe that divorce must occur even with these mismatches.* Why? Because no one's love style is cast in cement. We can learn to become more flexible in our own style of loving. We can adapt to our partner's style so that each person can experience the type of love he or she is seeking. I have seen it happen. I would also add, however, that some styles are healthier and more mature than others. People with a *Possessive* or *Game-playing* style must learn to develop other styles and discover fulfillment of other types of love. Such development is possible as we seek a greater understanding of the true meaning of the depth of love.

How can we change love styles? The presence of Jesus Christ in our lives. His presence enables us to refashion our own style of loving, even if it has been based upon childhood feelings of insecurity and rejection. Jesus Christ can fill the needs and lacks in our lives and free us to love in a biblical way. Our styles of loving can achieve needed balance.

As long as two people remain married they will need to define and redefine their styles of loving because our needs change over the years. When the communication lines are open and we learn to speak the other person's love language, love blossoms.

Now, here are the answers to the two questions I posed earlier. If you said that women are more likely to be *Logical, Possessive,* or *Best Friend* lovers, you were correct. Men score higher in *Game-playing* and *Romantic Love.* When it comes to *Unselfish Love,* there is no difference between the sexes.[7] Furthermore, according to researchers Lobsenz and Lasswell, a combination of *Best Friend* and *Unselfish* styles is as close to the ideal as a couple can get. Developing this blend calls for patience, sensitivity, availability, understanding, and acceptance by each partner for the other even when he/she does not express love in the same manner as you do.[8]

Love in Biblical Terms

We have considered contemporary descriptions of love; now let's consider what the Scripture says about it. The Greeks in the time of the New Testament used at least five words to identify and describe the various aspects of love in a marriage relationship. These biblical words can teach us much about loving one another as partners.

The first word to describe marital love is never translated "love" in the Bible, but it is a very important element of love. The word is *epithumia,* meaning a strong desire of any kind. It also means to set one's heart on, long for or even covet! Some desires are good and others are not. When *epithumia* is used in the Bible in a negative way, it is translated "lust." In a marriage relationship, *epithumia* is expressed in the strong physical desire a husband and wife have for each other which culminates in physical lovemaking. Sexual fulfillment in marriage is an important part of expressing and building love in a marriage.

Eros is a word for love that many individuals have heard, but few really understand. It is a Greek word, but it never appears in the New Testament, even though its Hebrew counterpart is found in the Old Testament. The Greeks used *eros* to describe normal sexual attraction and love. *Eros* is the root for our English word erotic.

Eros means devoted to, or tending to arouse, sexual love or desire. *Eros* defines someone who is strongly affected by sexual desire. *Eros* can be controlled and positive, or uncontrolled and sinful. It is not limited to the expression of sensual love, but also includes the desire to unite with and possess the loved one. For many, *eros* is the starting point for marriage. It conveys the idea of romance more than any other Greek term. If you would like to read more about *eros* love, I would suggest that you read the Song of Solomon in the Bible to discover the beauty of erotic love in a marriage.

As important as erotic love is, a relationship built solely on *eros* will not have the staying power it needs. Why? *Eros* is dependent upon feelings for its life. And even though erotic feelings can be intense and pleasurable, they can also be difficult to control. *Eros* is also dependent on the response of another person to keep it alive. If there is a lack of response, *eros* dies like a coal taken from a roaring fire. Furthermore, *eros* can be selfish and self-satisfying. And since it is based upon feelings, *eros* tends to be fragile and easily offended and hurt.

The Greek word *storge* depicts a third type of love. *Storge* denotes a sense of natural affection and of belonging to each other. Partners who find in each other assurance of loyalty and emotional refuge are experiencing *storge* love.

Fourth, *phileo* is friendship love, one of the highest priorities for marriage. *Phileo* means companionship, communication, cooperation and the sheer enjoyment of each other's presence. Thoughts, feelings, attitudes, experiences, and dreams are shared together. *Phileo* lovers cherish and enjoy each other completely.

Finally there is *agape* love, the highest expression of love in the Bible. *Agape* love values and serves the loved one. It is the love that keeps on loving even when the loved one becomes unlovable. *Agape* can keep erotic love alive or rekindle erotic love that has been quenched. *Agape* is the type of love that you make happen by a personal act of commitment. It is the love that most completely describes God's selfless, serving love commitment to us, as found in John 3:16 and 1 John 4:19, for example.

Rick Yohn has a great insight on the application of *agape* love in marriage:

> A husband who loves his wife as Christ loved (*agape*) the church will make every sacrifice to meet her needs (not necessarily all her wants). He will provide for her physical needs of sexual love, financial security, clothes, food, etc. He will provide for her emotional needs like security, affection, understanding, acceptance, the feeling of being wanted, and of feeling necessary to complete him. He will provide for her spiritual needs by encouraging her to grow in the Lord. He will set the example of what it means to walk in the Spirit.[9]

Agape is a love that is not based upon feelings but on an act of the will. And *agape* does not come from within you but from God. It will cost you something to love *agape* style. It is an art to be learned, but the pattern is seen throughout Scripture. It is also a discipline to be maintained by constant commitment and by drawing upon God for its sustenance.

Agape love is an unconditional love that is not based upon your spouse's performance. It is a love that says, "I love you in spite of...." *Agape* love is also transparent love. Transparency involves openness, honesty, truth, and sharing positive and negative feelings. *Agape* is strong enough to allow our partners to get close to us, even inside us. It is a love that has a deep reservoir to draw from and provides warmth and stability in the marriage even during times of stress and conflict.

Now that we've seen the biblical styles of love, let's evaluate their presence and strength in your marriage relationship as we did with the other love styles.

Draw a circle around the number that best indicates where you are on the scale for each Greek term (0 means non-existent, 10 means very strong). Then indicate, from your perspective, where your spouse is for each expression of love by drawing a square around the appropriate number:

Epithumia	1	2	3	4	5	6	7	8	9	10
Eros	1	2	3	4	5	6	7	8	9	10
Storge	1	2	3	4	5	6	7	8	9	10
Phileo	1	2	3	4	5	6	7	8	9	10
Agape	1	2	3	4	5	6	7	8	9	10

Which of these expressions of love would you like to see increased in your marriage?

What will you *do* to help this increase happen and when?

Remember that you can learn what love is from the Word of God. Love is very rational and you can understand it. Love is an art that needs to be cultivated and it is a power that can be controlled by your own will.

A Loving Relationship

What does it mean to love another person in terms of daily living? Here are a number of responses given by individuals who were asked to define a loving relationship:

"A loving relationship is a choice partnership. Loving someone in which even imperfection is seen as possibility and, therefore, a thing of beauty; where discovery, struggle and acceptance are the basis of continued growth and wonderment."

"A loving relationship is one in which individuals trust each other enough to become vulnerable, secure that the other person won't take advantage. It neither exploits nor takes the other for granted. It involves *much* communication, much sharing, and much tenderness."

"A loving relationship is one in which one can be open and honest with another without the fear of being judged. It's being secure in the knowledge that you are each other's best friend and no matter what happens you will stand by one another."

"A loving relationship is one which offers comfort in the silent presence of another with whom you know, through words or body language, you share mutual trust, honesty, admiration, devotion, and that special thrill of happiness simply being together."

"A loving relationship is an undemanding exchange of affection and concern, rooted in total honesty and continuing communication without exploitation."

"A loving relationship is one in which the loved one is free to be himself—to laugh with me, but never at me; to cry with me, but never because of me; to love life, to love himself, to love being loved. Such a relationship is based upon freedom and can never grow in a jealous heart."

"A loving relationship is one in which each one sees the beloved not as an extension of self but as a unique, forever becoming, beautiful individual—a situation in which the persons can bring their own special I to each other, a blending of selves without the fear of loss of self."[10]

What is love in marriage all about? First of all, it is an unconditional commitment to an imperfect person! Most people do not understand commitment when they are married because they do not yet realize how imperfect their partner is. Commitment means you thank God for your partner in spite of the imperfections you discover. You also thank Him for your spouse's acceptance of *your* imperfections! Married love remains stable regardless of circumstances.

In order to love you must be willing to run the risk of being hurt, rejected or feeling unloved. Love means wanting the best for your partner and seeing him/her as a friend rather than an enemy. Love means sensing, encouraging and supporting each other's dreams. Love means wanting your partner to become all that he or she can be even if you are threatened by his/her progress! And love means giving security when your partner needs security and giving space when he/she needs space.

In light of the various ideas and definitions of love given so far, complete the following sentences:

1. The way in which I would like to give love to my spouse is...

2. The way in which I would like to receive love from my spouse is...

3. The specific ways in which I could show my love even more are...

4. The specific ways in which my spouse could show his/ her love more are...

5. What I really appreciate about the way my spouse loves me is...

No matter how deep your love for your spouse may be, it will be unknown to him/her unless it is openly and consistently expressed in a manner that registers with your partner. Far too many marriage partners are silent and passive in their expressions of love. God has called us to be vessels of love pouring generously to our partners. Marriage is God's creative gift to us, providing us the opportunity to express love to its fullest in the safety and security of an abiding relationship. And we are only able to love because He first loved us. His love is so extensive that it can heal the loveless experiences of the past. We no longer need to be dominated by hurtful memories. Instead we can live and love knowing the adequacy of Jesus Christ in our lives.

So liberating is this miracle of loving and being loved that it is something of which a husband and wife will take great joy in reminding one another. Indeed, one of the most important tasks for a couple to fulfill is this work of telling one another their love, which at heart is the wonderful reminder that they each are loved by God. This will not always be a pleasant or an easy task: sometimes, to be sure, when a wife says, "I love you," it is something that a husband does not want to hear, at times something that he almost cannot bear to hear. He is tired of hearing it. He doesn't want to think about what it means. He does not want to let go of whatever it is that is preventing him from accepting it. He doesn't have the time or the energy to make a response. He doesn't want to be bothered with it. It is one more responsibility he can do without. He is not in the mood to be loved, let alone to love anyone else.

Still, in spite of all resistance, the words of love are important. It is important that they be heard, and it is important that they be spoken, out loud, no matter how painful this hearing and this speaking might be. It is a marvelous thing when love comes bubbling up like tears in the throat as one is gripped by a sudden stabbing realization of the other's beauty and goodness, of how incredibly precious they are.[11]

The poet Lois Wyse, in her book, *Lovetalk*, puts it this way:

> I remember how I met you.
> I guess everybody who loves somebody remembers how they
>   met.
> I remember the first time I saw you.
> That is the key word:
> Saw.
> I saw you.
> Love starts with a look,
> A meeting of the eyes that locks two people in understanding.
> I melted. Just a little. Not so anyone could notice.
> From then on there was excitement,
> Anticipation for the next meeting.
> And before long I was propelled into deeper emotional
>   waters.
> Nonverbal.
> The whole thing was nonverbal.
> But could I have continued to fantasize
> If we had never talked?
> Many people distrust words, and for good reason.
> We have all been deceived by words.
> We have all failed at some time
> To say precisely what we meant because
> We could not find the proper word.
> How many times have I shrugged my shoulders,
> Smiled sheepishly, and said,
> Oh, you know what I mean.
> But do you?
> I mean if you don't really know what is in my head
> When I can't express
> Dum dum things like going to the store or hanging a shelf,
> How are you supposed to know what I mean when I talk
>   about things we cannot see?[12]

We will all experience different seasons in our marriages and the intensity of love will change over the years. You may have intense feelings of love now, but the intensity could waver from weakness to even greater strength as the years pass. That's the way feelings are. But don't be threatened by wavering feelings, because true love can endure a lifetime of them. As Booth Tarkington put it:

It is love in old age, no longer blind, that is true love. For love's highest intensity doesn't necessarily mean its highest quality. Glamour and jealousy are gone; and the ardent caress, no longer needed, is valueless compared to the reassuring touch of a trembling hand. Passers-by commonly see little beauty in the embrace of young lovers on a park bench, but the understanding smile of an old wife to her husband is one of the loveliest things in the world.[13]

Notes

1. John Souter, *Love* (Wheaton, IL: Tyndale House Publishers, 1986), adapted from pp. 2-5.
2. Source unknown.
3. Scott M. Peck, *The Road Less Traveled* (New York: Simon and Schuster, Inc., 1978), p. 91. Used by permission.
4. Leo F. Buscaglia, *Loving Each Other* (New York: Random House, Inc., Fawcett Columbine, 1984), pp. 18,19. Used by permission.
5. Marcia Lasswell and Norman N. Lobsenz, *Styles of Loving: Why You Love the Way You Do* (New York: Doubleday and Co., Inc., 1980), adapted from pp. 85-103.
6. Ibid., pp. 167-168.
7. Ibid., adapted from p. 105.
8. Ibid., adapted from pp. 113-114.
9. Rick Yohn, *Beyond Spiritual Gifts* (Wheaton, IL: Tyndale House Publishers, 1976), pp. 27-28.
10. Leo F. Buscaglia, *Loving Each Other*, pp. 46-50. Used by permission.
11. Mike Mason, *The Mystery of Marriage: As Iron Sharpens Iron* (Portland, OR: Multnomah Press, 1986), p. 65. Used by permission.
12. "Lovetalk" by Lois Wyse from LOVETALK. Copyright © 1973 by Lois Wyse. Reprinted by permission of Doubleday & Company, Inc., pp. 23-24.
13. Original source unknown.

~FIVE~
Where Did the
Romance Go?

They sat in my office side by side, removing handwritten sheets from their packets. This engaged couple was ready to begin sharing their responses to an important question they had been asked prior to their initial premarital counseling session. Each of them had been asked to write down 12 specific reasons why they wanted to marry their intended life partner.

I sat and listened as the woman, in her 30s, read to her fiancé her list of reasons for wanting to marry him. Some of her reasons were:

1. My life is now complete because of Jim. Everything I lacked before meeting him is now fulfilled. And I can look forward to being fulfilled for the rest of my life.

2. God has led me to the one person He has selected for me. I know Jim is that one person and I could not be happy with any other person.

3. The attention he gives me, with his emphasis on "little things," is a delight. I have never experienced such attentiveness before.

4. He must be the one for me since I think about him so much and in such a positive way.

5. He wants us to have the type of marriage I have always dreamed of but have never seen happen, even in my own parents' marriage.

6. My life was sort of humdrum and in a rut for the past several years. Now Jim has added new meaning to life and I want that to continue.

This woman's reasons for marrying Jim are important because they reflect her personal values and state what is important to her. Her reasons also communicate the message, "I don't ever want you to change. I want our relationship to continue as is."

What thoughts come to your mind as you read the reasons listed above? Are this woman's hopes for marriage realistic? Are her expectations too high? Will she be disappointed in time? Are her reasons appropriately balanced between romanticism and realism?

Let's consider another set of reasons I heard recently, stating why a 40-year-old man wanted to marry his fiancée, Judy:

1. Because she is truly special! Unique! Just right for me. She's not perfect, mind you. But then, neither am I. And I don't need someone perfect. I need and want her.

2. I have a great deal of respect for her: for her spirituality and her purity and holiness. Although we have struggled in this area, we have been successful in establishing a relationship of purity.

3. She truly does actively minister to me and bless me. She *cares* for me! And she enjoys it and is blessed by giving to me and ministering to me! She believes that I am someone special.

4. I can successfully bless her and minister to her and I love it!!

5. She is such a very feminine woman!! She is beautiful and she enjoys being a lovely woman. She does this for herself and for me.

6. We are sexually compatible. We are both cuddly, enjoy hugging and are affectionate. We love to touch, hug, kiss, hold hands, embrace. We have been able to talk openly about sex and our desires and wishes.

7. She is so expressive to me verbally. We communicate very well. We have developed a way to talk about even difficult/awkward/painful/sensitive topics without ever calling into question our love and dedication to each other.

8. We have been through a few tough events, have worked through them well and are getting better at it as time goes by.

Both of these lists reflect the desire of engaged couples for romance in their marriages. The second list suggests that Judy and her fiancé are a very romantic, affectionate and thoroughly realistic couple who will be able to weather the adjustments and changes of marriage. But the

---

As the rains of reality and the winds of stress blow upon the dream-world marriage, the relationship that was to last "forever" quickly crumbles.

---

list given by Jim's intended bride shows a potentially dangerous preoccupation with romance at the expense of a realistic view of the marriage relationship.

The Thrill Is Gone

Some time after the honeymoon, many married couples ask, "What happened to the magic? It's disappeared. We were romantic at one time—where did it go? It's almost like an illusive dream. Does this happen to everyone?" Yes, all marriages change with time and courtship-level romance often fades. Depending on the couple, romance can either disappear completely or it can change with the marriage and be expressed in new, more creative ways.

For many of us, romance and marriage was the pot of gold at the end of our childhood rainbow of grown-up fantasies. Most marital journeys begin with some romantic intentions. Some of these intentions are sky high while others are just a bit above the horizon. And in some marriages, each partner has different aspirations for romance; this difference can create strain on the marriage and disappointment in one or both partners.

As most of us moved toward marriage, our sense of reality was distorted by wishfulness and fantasy. Often this intense romantic illusion can neutralize the positive development of the marriage. The fantasies and unrealistic expectations brought to marriage can create a gulf between the spouses as the disappointments mount up.

Many marriages are like houses built upon sand—they are weakly founded upon romantic dreams. When we dream our minds do not have to distinguish between reality and fantasy, so we are able to create without restraint. There is nothing wrong with dreams because they are often starting points for successful endeavors. But dreams that are not followed by adequate planning usually do not come true in the real world.

Any marriage built predominantly upon dreams is a high risk since dreams do not consider the disappointments and changes that are inevitable in every marriage. Romance does change in time. As the rains of reality and the winds of stress blow upon the dream-world marriage, the relationship that was to last "forever" quickly crumbles. Much more is involved in fulfilling romantic dreams than merely expecting them to come true.

Dr. Mark Lee describes the dream process:

> Fantasy-making is a form of self-entertainment by which dreams presume life is made bearable in circumstances which are less than they anticipated. Fantasy is a defense mechanism. Fantasies serve by helping people live with inequities and disappointments. We know that unrestrained thought patterns create larger dimensions for life than human beings can fulfill. Man's inability to accomplish what he can conjure seems less objectionable to him when he creates fairy tales about himself.
>
> The Christian may use imagination for creativity, ending ultimately in the realization of heaven, or he can use it for lesser purposes, even false ones. Imposing blissful fantasies upon a

marriage commonly makes for psychological aggression, forcing on a spouse expectations he cannot achieve. Even so, modest fantasies may help marriages, if they are employed to improve legitimate relationships. Fantasies may intensify worthwhile reality experiences. As in so many other matters, fantasies may be blessings or cursings.[1]

Where Did the Thrill Go?

Let's consider what happens to romance in marriage, why there is a change and what can be done about it.

If you married in your early 20s, as most couples do, you married at a time when most individuals are in the midst of developing their own personal lives. You are still in the process of establishing your own identity. You are still trying to discover "who you are." Your self-discovery can often be overshadowed by the attraction you and your loved one feel for each other and your desire for marriage.

Think back to your courtship for example. What thoughts and feelings went through your mind and heart? Most of us started our marital journey by falling in love. And if you think back to determine how it happened, you might be hard pressed to come up with an answer. You just know that it *did* happen. Do you remember when your thoughts strayed all day long to your loved one and your pulse quickened when you saw him or her? For some, love and romance was a growing process and for others it was like a jolt of electricity.

We act differently when we are in love and sometimes to others we even appear odd. We don't really care what others think if we dance around the car holding each other close, or receive a four-foot high romantic greeting card from that special person while in the midst of teaching 30 high school students. Feelings of abandon and delight are common. Praise the Lord! There is nothing wrong with romantic feelings during courtship (perhaps they are still happening).

Marriage does need a sense of delight, excitement, romance and mystery. The problem lies in expecting every moment of every day to be lived in that fashion. We began our marriages with the conviction that our spouse was the right one for us and that feelings of love and romance were there to help convince us of that fact. Healthy romance is a balance of both feelings and thoughts. And some of us rely more upon one than the other.

Learning to love another person for life may involve idealizing and projecting—psychological exercises that can distort true romance and

---

Couples unprepared for changes in romance will eventually begin to question whether or not they are really in love in the first place.

---

love. Idealization means seeing another person as we wish him/her to be. And projection means mentally imposing an ideal image, created in our minds, upon the real person. What happens when we idealize or project? Tremendous disillusionment, disappointment and frustration will result after only a few months of marriage because the real person can never live up to our flawless ideal.

I do not agree with those who say that romance is the enemy of marriage. Many decry romance as an irrational, selfish, emotional high that creates fantasies and unrealistic expectations that no mortal person could ever fulfill. Yes, the passionate attraction between a couple that we call romantic love can generate an intense ecstasy. And it is true that frustrated romance can also generate tremendous suffering. Many call romance a false hope because of the tragedy, confusion and disappointment that sometimes accompany it.

But romantic frustration and suffering are not the fault of romance per se. The fault lies in a lack of balance in some individuals' lives. Some people look to romance as the panacea for the lack of satisfaction, low self-esteem and lack of personal identity they are experiencing in their own lives. They bring to their romance defects and weaknesses instead of strengths. Thus they expect too much of romance.

The second culprit of romantic disillusionment is failing to see romantic feelings as only the first step in a relationship. Couples must understand, anticipate and plan for the many changes that will occur in their relationship. The romantic love which brought a man and a woman together will evolve into something with less ecstasy but greater depth. Failing to realize the inevitability of change is the greatest cause for hurt in marriage. Couples unprepared for changes in romance will eventually begin to question whether or not they are really in love in the first place.

James Olthius gives us the following healthy perspective on romance:

> One essential ingredient of a good marriage is romance—not adolescent infatuation, but the steady delight and genuine sparkle of two people who enjoy and nurture each other.
>
> Romance is not all of married love, but it is its indispensable emotional component. Without romance, not as a constant state of arousal, but as a general feeling of comfort, pleasure, and delight, a marriage is destined to be a listless, dry, and dreary relationship, no matter how strong the commitment. Without the emotional connection we call romance, a marriage lacks the zest and excitement that leads to satisfaction. Married couples, if all is well, experience this connection in a host of unsung and uneventful ways, as well as in the moments of intense passion, waves of tenderness, or candles and soft music. A marriage without such connection is a divorce waiting to happen.[2]

The challenge of marriage is discovering romance, anticipating its maturing change through the years and keeping it alive!

Marital Stages and Changes

All marriages change because all people change. But do the changes in our marriages just happen or do we have something to say about them?

All marriages enter into phases or stages. The changes that occur in these stages are not necessarily good or bad, but they are a reality. Some changes come upon us without warning or choice on our part. But there are other changes that we can control by personal choice. We can choose not to plan for changes in our marriage. We can instead dream that our storybook romance will always be this way or believe that we are stuck with our less-than-ideal marriage the way it is. With this attitude any changes that do occur are "beyond our control." The rationale seems to be, "If we do nothing, our marriage will change naturally for the better." And if it doesn't change for the better, we can always blame our spouse.

David and Vera Mace suggest that we need to expect our marriages to change:

> We need to see marriage in new terms, as a continually growing, continually changing, interaction between a man and a woman who are seeking warmth and richness of the shared life. Marriage has too often been portrayed as two people frozen together side by side, as immobile as marble statues. More accurately, it is the intricate and graceful cooperation of two dancers who through long practice have learned to match each other's movements and moods in response to the music of the spheres.[3]

Growth can be painful and most of us resist it in one way or another. Even emotionally healthy couples resist growth at first, but then learn to nourish joint development and growth. Too often it is immature people who resist the growth and changes of marriage the most. Unfortunately there is a high price tag for such resistance.

There are many ways to view the stages or growth periods of marriage. I like the manner in which Maxine Rock identifies the stages of marriage, applicable to Christians and non-Christians alike. Her thoughts, adapted from her book, *The Marriage Map,* provide the structure for the rest of the chapter.[4] I have included additional thoughts for each stage, especially the beginning stages of marriage.

Stage one of marriage is called *Fantasy Time* and ranges from the first to the third year. This is when you tend to think everything about your spouse is wonderful. If you find any faults during this period, they are cute rather than annoying. This foggy stage of marriage is often called the "honeymoon period." For some this dreamy stage is over within three months!

> Auto mechanics tell us that the way a car is treated in the first thousand miles will have a deep and lasting influence on the way it behaves later. Something like that is true also of the marriage relationship. We now know that the shape of a marriage develops quite early. In the first six or twelve months a couple develops habits of behaving toward one another that become settled and are not easily changed later.
>
> These habits decide a number of important questions: who plays the dominant and who the submissive role, who takes major responsibility for the different areas of the couple's shared life, how quarrels are handled, who initiates the first move to make up, who makes the final decision in what areas, how household chores are allocated, how money is managed, how sexual needs are met, how leisure time is spent.[5]

Have You Met the Challenges?

Let's consider some of the challenges for a couple during the first year of marriage. "But wait a minute!" you say. "This doesn't apply to us because we've been married much longer than one year." Please read on. Many couples who have been married for 20 years or more have not made all these adjustments.

There are seven crucial challenges in the initial six months of any marriage. After reading the description of each challenge, evaluate your success as a couple by completing the exercise provided.

1. Define terms. An important challenge for newlyweds is to define the terms "husband" and "wife" in such a way that they can remain close together as a loving couple and yet exist as separate individuals. It is important that each retains his/her individual identity while drawing close together as a couple. A marriage relationship is meant to be a freeing-up to develop uniqueness and spiritual giftedness in his or her own way, and join these to give the marital relationship strength and greater potential. This may mean breaking loose from preconceived images each one has of what a wife or husband should be. If couples cannot allow each other to develop, grow and be creative in defining new roles, the conflict will be intense. As one author so vividly puts it, "Both of you will wind up drilling holes in your own marriage before it has left the shore."[6]

On a scale of one to ten, with ten being high, how well have you accomplished this task?

1   2   3   4   5   6   7   8   9   10

In what way can Jesus Christ make a difference at this stage?

2. Understand differences. Another challenge is to view interpersonal differences as the expression of attitudes rather than as signs of rejection or loss of love. Appreciation for uniqueness must replace any threat of competition.

How well have you accomplished this task?

1   2   3   4   5   6   7   8   9   10

In what way can Jesus Christ make a difference at this stage?

3. Delineate between families. Married couples must create new relationships with their respective families of origin in order to establish an independent life as a couple and still maintain a loving, guilt-free, warm connection with their parents. You must break the child-to-parent ties and reestablish them as an adult-to-adult relationship. A person needs to complete the separation process from his/her parents for a marriage to properly develop. One must "leave" in order to properly "cleave," as stated in Genesis 2:24. By making peace with one's parents and separating completely, a man/woman can be at peace with himself/herself and thus also with a marriage partner.

How well have you accomplished this task?

1   2   3   4   5   6   7   8   9   10

In what way can Jesus Christ make a difference at this stage?

4. Move from courtship love to married love. Couples must differentiate courtship love from married love so they can develop their capacity to value and appreciate the qualities of married love, which are different from courtship love. You need to develop the romantic love of courtship into a love based upon steady commitment. Before you marry you may be drawn to your friend because of a specific character trait which you see as a strength. After marriage you may find that this "strength" begins to bother you. You begin to view it as a weakness and want your partner to change. Character traits, however, are expressions of personality. If traits bother you, they need to be discussed, not attacked as a weakness. Labeling a neutral behavior as a weakness does little to bring about desired change.

The love that is needed to stabilize a marriage is the type of love God displays to each of us—unconditional commitment to an imperfect person. Unconditional love takes energy and effort. It means caring about the other person as much as you care about yourself. Mel Krantzler describes what marital love actually means:

> Marital love requires the ability to put yourself in your partner's place, to understand that the differences that divide you are the differences of two unique personalities, rather than betrayals of your hopes and dreams. The unconditional willingness of each of you to understand and resolve these differences through the sharing of your deepest feelings, concerns, attitudes and ideas is a fundamental component of marital love. Postponement of your need for instant gratification when your partner feels no such need; sharing the struggle to triumph over adversities as well as sharing the joys and delights of being together; nurturing each other in defeat caused by forces beyond our control and renewing each other's courage to prevail in the face of despair; carrying necessary obligations and responsibilities as a flower rather than as a hundred-pound knapsack; acknowledging the everyday value of your partner in a look, a smile, a touch of the hand, a voiced appreciation of a meal or a new hair style, a spontaneous trip to a movie or a restaurant; trusting your partner always has your best interests at heart even when criticism is given; loyalty and dedication to each other in the face of sacrifices that may have to be made— all of these are additional components of marital love that courtship knows little about.[7]

How well have you accomplished this task?

     1   2   3   4   5   6   7   8   9   10

In what way can Jesus Christ make a difference at this stage?

5. Keep finances in perspective. The clash of two philosophies of money management can be a prime source of marital friction. Early

married couples must decide never to let money problems erode their trust and love for each other.
How well have you accomplished this task?

1   2   3   4   5   6   7   8   9   10

In what way can Jesus Christ make a difference at this stage?

6. Learn from each other. Neither partner in a marriage possesses all wisdom, knowledge or ability. Each must occupy the dual roles of friendly teacher and receptive student to each other.
How well have you accomplished this task?

1   2   3   4   5   6   7   8   9   10

In what way can Jesus Christ make a difference at this stage?

7. Choose to blend. A critical challenge to couples is to create a caring marital environment in which each partner is more concerned with give than take. Caring couples practice voluntary modification of inappropriate behavior in place of a power-struggle atmosphere in which winning and losing are of paramount importance.
How well have you accomplished this task?

1   2   3   4   5   6   7   8   9   10

In what way can Jesus Christ make a difference at this stage?

Describe how you adjusted to and worked through the *Fantasy*

Time stage of your marriage. If you are still in this stage or have not faced it yet, what will you do to adjust?

Stage two of marriage has been described as <u>Compromise and</u> ranges from year two to year seven. During this stage the couple encounters mutual disappointment. Each partner realizes that he/she is annoyed or hurt by his/her spouse's traits and habits. In fact, this can be the first time that signs of marital burnout occur. Most couples begin to work for compromise, each partner persuading the other to change and promising to make changes in return. But it is also during this very dangerous stage that many couples throw in the towel and divorce.

Let's look at the elements that can douse the marital flame during this second stage. No marriage is 100 percent ecstasy. However, if you detect a pattern of anger and resentment developing toward your mate, check the following burnout signals to see where you stand. Give yourself five points for every yes response to the following questions:

Have you...
- found yourself looking for excuses to leave or stay away from the house?
- quit caring about your appearance when your spouse is due home?
- no interests or hobbies in common?
- quit laughing with your spouse?
- stopped meeting your spouse with a smile when he/she gets home?
- changed your sleeping habits?
- lost interest in having the house neat and clean inside and out?
- made more visits to your doctor this past year than in previous years?

Do you...
- and your spouse have fewer and fewer couple friends?
- and your spouse have little interest in each other's work?
- no longer compliment your spouse?
- resent your spouse's family and friends?
- often feel angry?
- think members of the singles' Sunday School group have more fun than you do?
- spend time planning activities for yourself that don't include your spouse?
- sleep in separate bedrooms when neither of you even snores?
- feel less sexually attractive?
- and your spouse only communicate on a factual level?

Now total your points and check your score against the scale. Where are you? And where is your mate?

MARITAL BURNOUT SCALE

0-25—Still some fire left; continue to fan the flame.

30-50—Not enough oxygen; your marital flame is smothering; turn up the gas!

55-75—Heading for a black-out; you and your mate have your work cut out for you.

80-100—Ashes! Professional help needed fast![8]

Describe how you adjusted to and worked through the *Compromise* stage of your marriage. If you are still in this stage or have not faced it yet, what will you do to adjust?

Stage three of marriage is labeled *Reality Struggles* and can range from year five to year ten. During this stage you realize that some of the changes you desire will occur, but there will be other areas in which neither you nor your spouse will change much at all. You and your spouse are limited, imperfect people. Neither of you can live up to the other's expectations. You must learn to understand and accept the imperfections of your partner.

This is also the time of life when permanent bonding occurs. Unfortunately, more couples stay together because of children and financial dependency than because of intensive love and commitment.

Describe how you adjusted to and worked through the *Reality Struggles* stage of your marriage. If you are still in this stage or have not faced it yet, what will you do to adjust?

Stage four of marriage is the time of *Decisions,* usually occurring from year 10 to year 15. At this stage we accept the reality of the relationship but often have mixed feelings about it. We realize that some of our spouse's bad points are here to stay, but may wonder if the good points are sufficient to make up for the bad. A major question at this time is, "Can I (or do I want to) make the changes necessary to adjust to my partner's unchangeable areas so these conflicts don't interfere with the ongoing growth of the marriage?"

Of course, a person's attitude at this stage makes a difference in answering these decision-making questions. Knowing Jesus Christ as personal Lord makes the greatest difference. The Holy Spirit can do radical surgery on our attitudes and behavior if we allow Him to.

Describe how you adjusted to and worked through the *Decisions* stage of your marriage. If you are still in this stage or have not faced it yet, what will you do to adjust?

Stage five, sometimes called *Separation,* occurs for most couples from year 14 to year 20, but is manifested in different ways. For some couples, the major struggle is deciding whether to stay together, adjust, cope, and put forth the effort needed to make the marriage work, or to separate and divorce. Separation can occur even when couples stay together. Many married partners act like married singles in attitude and behavior toward one another. Some of you may be "separated" in attitude and your spouse is oblivious to it.

This stage is one of the most painful times in the marriage journey. It ends when the couple starts talking about specific ways to change their lives in order to make the marriage work. In many cases it takes some type of crisis for marriage-saving dialog to occur. And when the effort begins, there is relief in knowing that your partner cares enough to work through the problem. The painful experience of rescuing a marriage can lead to a deep level of commitment.

Describe how you adjusted to and worked through the *Separation* stage of your marriage. If you are still in this stage or have not faced it yet, what will you do to adjust?

Stage six is called *Together Again.* This stage occurs when, in spite of what has taken place in the marriage and the areas of difference between them, a couple realizes that they want to remain married. The renewed commitment is to the opposite spouse and to the ongoing growth of the marriage as well. Separation and divorce are no longer options.

Describe how you adjusted to and worked through the *Together Again* stage of your marriage. If you are still in this stage or have not faced it yet, what will you do to adjust?

The seventh and last stage of marriage is called _New Freedom_ and often occurs from year 20 to year 25 and beyond. Each partner is released from the pressures of trying so hard and the relationship flows more comfortably. Each partner feels accepted and is much more accepting. Individual growth has a greater opportunity to occur at this time because both partners are free to explore new ways of fulfilling themselves. Marital satisfaction during these years increases for many.

Describe how you adjusted to and worked through the *New Freedom* stage of your marriage. If you are still in this stage or have not faced it yet, what will you do to adjust?

Congratulations! You have survived the first half of the book. Let's continue by discovering how to rid your marriage of a major romance killer and by learning how to increase love, romance and intimacy with your spouse.

Notes
1. Mark Lee, *Time Bombs in Marriage* (Chappaqua, NY: Christian Herald Association, 1981), p. 16.
2. James H. Olthius, *Keeping Our Troth* (San Francisco: Harper and Row, Publishers, Inc., 1986), p. 53.
3. David and Vera Mace, *We Can Have Better Marriages If We Really Want Them* (Nashville: Abingdon Press, 1974), p. 144. Used by permission.
4. Maxine Rock, *The Marriage Map* (Atlanta, GA: Peachtree Publishers, 1986), adapted from pp. 39-41.
5. Source unknown.
6. Mel Krantzler, *Creative Marriages* (New York: McGraw-Hill Book Company, 1981), p. 50.
7. Krantzler, *Creative Marriages*, p. 54.
8. Nancy Badgewell, "To Rekindle the Marital Fire," *Dynamic Years*, (September-October, 1985), pp. 28,29.

—SIX—
Ridding Your Romance of Resentment

*W*e have an abundance of insects in California. One type is rarely seen but it definitely makes its presence known. It is the destructive termite. Hidden from view, the termite slowly and steadily continues to feast its way through the skeletal structure of a house month after month. Some homeowners may be aware of termites as telltale indications of infestation are discovered from time to time. But too many ignore the warning signs and fail to take appropriate steps to evict the invaders.

The subtle erosion continues and eventually the damage becomes apparent and the problem can no longer be ignored. But by the time the termites' work has reached the visible surface, the internal damage is extensive and major repairs and expensive reconstruction are often necessary.

The Termites of a Marriage

In marriage, the destructive counterpart to the unseen termite is resentment. An insidious disease, this feeling of ill will is a barrier to the growth of romance and intimacy as well as being a corrosive acid that eats away at the existing relationship. Resentment is usually bred from a real or imagined hurt that we hold against the perpetrator. The resentful heart operates like a bill collection agency, making the person pay again and again for what we believe he or she has done. But we often charge so much interest that, no matter how earnestly the other person tries to pay the debt, there always seems to be a balance held against them.

Resentment costs both parties; it hurts the offender and the offendee. But the greatest damage is done to the relationship. In any war, many innocent parents are killed and an abundance of orphans are the result. The marital relationship becomes the orphan as the two spouses engage in their war dance of resentment. Termite exterminators often say, "If you would have called us sooner, it would have been much easier and less expensive to eliminate the problem." So it is with resentment that is not dealt with early.

In marriage there will always be disappointments, hurts and unmet needs and expectations. After all, you married an imperfect person— and, by the way, so did your spouse! But instead of forgiving a spouse's failures, the resenting spouse says, "You hurt me! You owe me! You must pay! I will get even with you!" But you can never get even. Lewis Smedes says, "Revenge never evens the score, for alienated people never keep score of wrongs by the same mathematics."[1]

Bill, who has been married for three years, is upset. "I'm so mad," he says. "My wife doesn't know what a compliment is! She never notices what I do, and I feel she takes all my work around the house for granted! She should have married a construction engineer."

And Janice, who has been married for a year now, tearfully says, "My husband is so insensitive. I'm not sure he realizes what marriage is all about. Demands and crude remarks are his forte! Just wait until the next time he wants to get cozy!"

These people have obviously been offended. Altercations, differences and offenses frequently occur between individuals, families and even nations. Apologies, clarification of issues, truces, and peace treaties make it possible for individuals and nations to live their lives unhindered and unaffected by conflict. But does peace really occur? Does a resolution of differences really take place? Or is superficial peace and harmony tainted by lingering inner resentment?

Nations often agree to stop their hostilities and sign peace treaties. But peacemaking formalities do not necessarily change warlike attitudes. Years after the end of World War I, seething resentment eventually fanned the flames of World War II.

Your spouse may apologize and even give you a gift to show his or her good intentions. And you say, "Oh, that's all right. Let's just forget

---

Forgiveness costs. But the price tag of resentment demands continual payments.

---

it happened." But inwardly you still feel cold and unforgiving. And the iceberg of resentment freezes both intimacy and romance!

Harboring resentments can be an indication of unresolved hurts from your past. Perhaps you feel there were significant individuals or groups in your past who ignored, belittled, abandoned, or in some way attacked you. Have you forgiven them? Keeping past hurts in mind may breed resentment toward those in your life at the present time—like a marriage partner. You may think you have buried some of the bad memories in your subconscious mind. Then one day they come out unexpectedly, when you encounter a person or a situation that resembles the past experience. And you wonder, *Why did I react like that?*

There is a saying, "What you resist persists." It means if you are unwilling to let loose of the past, especially your resentment, get set for a repeat performance in some other way. Your emotional upset will reappear in some other form. For example, if the person you resent is your parent, you may find that your marriage partner, for some strange reason, begins to resemble the parent you resent. Or you may begin to act like the parent you never wanted to be like. You start behaving like that parent and treating others in the same way your parent treated you. You may even find that you experience some of the same illnesses or emotional upheavals your resented parent experienced. I have seen all these characteristics emerge in the various people with whom I work in counseling.

Fighting painful memories, bitterness and resentment takes a lot of energy. Because of this energy drain, people tend to respond to others in one of two unhealthy ways. For fear of another bad relationship, they hesitate to be open and intimate with anyone, protecting themselves with a wall of aloofness. Or they may be so starved for love, affection and acceptance that they are too open or intimate in their relationships. Both responses exert undue pressures on a marriage.

Do You Really Want Out?

Many couples I have counseled have said, "Norm, I know that it would be better to let go of these feelings and resentments, and forgive—but how do I do this?"

The question you must ask yourself is, Do I want to let go of my resentments or do I want revenge? Many married individuals struggle with letting their partner off the hook by forgiving them. With one foot on the road to forgiveness and the other on the road to revenge, you are immobilized. Why not make a commitment one way or the other? Why divide your energy? Why be half-hearted?

If the part of you that wants revenge against your partner is stronger than the forgiving part, then how are you going to get revenge? Does your partner know of your resentment? Is he/she aware of your craving for some kind of vengeance? Have you written out your plan of attack, with specific details of what you will do? Have you bluntly told your spouse about your feelings and your plans to get back at him/her? If not, why not? If revenge is what you want, why not get it over with and free yourself so your life can be full and unrestricted?

Your reaction is probably, "What? You're crazy! What a ridiculous idea! How could you suggest such a radical and thoroughly unbiblical idea? I would never want to do that, and even if I wanted to, I couldn't do it." Really? Then why not embrace the other alternative, give up your resentment completely and be washed clean of your resentful feelings?

Giving up your resentments may also involve giving up having someone else to blame for the predicaments you are in, feeling sorry for yourself, and talking negatively about the other person. You're right, forgiveness costs. But the price tag of resentment demands continual payments.

And think about this: When you hold resentment for someone, you have given him/her control of your emotional state. How do you feel about that? Most of us want to feel like we're in control of our emotions. But you are not in control if you resent someone! You have shifted the power source to someone else. You are letting another person push your emotional buttons of anger, frustration and bitterness. Instead, give control of your feelings to Jesus Christ and allow Him to work in your life.

The first step in relinquishing resentments is to become aware of and identify them. The second step is to forgive yourself for whatever you may have done to others. The third step is to forgive the significant people of your past for being who they were (and perhaps still are) and doing what they did. Please remember that these steps are easier said than done and they will take time.

What are some of the benefits of deciding to forgive your partner? Love, intimacy and romance can happen. And love frees you to disagree with what another person says or does without becoming resentful. You can even learn to communicate in an honest way. The change in your attitude may help the other person change.

Releasing Resentment

There are numerous ways to overcome and release resentment. In my counseling I use an approach that incorporates some of the better techniques currently practiced by therapists.[2] These suggestions can also be effective for you. And if your marriage is hindered because of hurts from the past, these techniques can be effective in releasing resentment whether the person(s) involved is living or deceased.

Begin by completing the following steps in writing. First, list all the resentments you hold toward your partner. Itemize each hurt or pain you can recall in as much detail as possible. Write down exactly what happened and how you felt about it then and now.

One client shared the following list of resentments:

I feel hurt that you made sarcastic remarks about me in front of others.

I feel hurt that you found it hard to ever give me approval.

I resent that you wouldn't listen to me.

Another one of my clients shared:

I hate the fact that you called me trash and treated me the same.

I feel offended by the way you try to use me for your own benefit.

I resent your not loving me for who I am. You're always trying to change me into some unreal image.

Please be aware that you may experience some emotional turmoil as you make your list. Many have shared that, as they face the resentments they hold toward their spouse, other old, buried feelings and experiences from their childhood come to mind. You may need to repeat this exercise for others in your past.

Prior to and during this writing exercise, ask God to reveal to you the deep hidden pools of memory so your entire inner container of resentment can be emptied. Thank Him that it is all right for you to wade through and expel these feelings. Visualize Jesus Christ in your mind's eye present in the room with you, smiling and giving His approval to what you are doing. Imagine Him saying to you, "I want you to be cleansed and free. You no longer need to be emotionally crippled because of what happened to you."

After you have thoroughly verbalized your resentments in writing, spend time formulating how you will share this with your spouse. Practice reading your list aloud. Then select an appropriate time to discuss the list with your partner. But be sure you share with him/her how you would appreciate being treated in the future. Always point toward the desired positive behaviors.

For some individuals it is too difficult to share a list of resentments with their partner. If it is so for you, employ an intermediate approach of sharing your list when your spouse is not present. Prepare a quiet, comfortable room with two chairs facing each other. Spend a few moments in prayer asking for the guidance of the Holy Spirit and the presence of Jesus Christ. Imagine Jesus coming into the room, walking up to you, smiling at you and telling you that He loves you and your partner, and that He wants you to be free from your resentments. He encourages you to proceed.

Sit down in one of the chairs and imagine that your spouse is sitting in the other. Begin reading your list to the other chair as if your spouse were there. As you read, imagine that your spouse is thoughtfully accepting what you are verbally sharing. Imagine him/her actually hearing you, nodding in acceptance and understanding your feelings.

At first you may feel awkward and even embarrassed about reading to an empty chair. But these feelings will pass. You may find yourself expanding on what you have written in the process of reading your list. You may become very intense, angry, depressed, or anxious as you rehearse these details aloud. Be sure to verbalize these feelings, too, in as much detail as possible. Remember, not only is your non-present spouse giving you permission to share all of your feelings, but Jesus is also there encouraging you to get these inner resentments out.

You may find that talking through only one topic of resentment will be enough for you to handle at one time. If you find yourself becoming emotionally drained, then stop, rest and relax. Resume the normal tasks of the day and come back to your list of resentments another time when you are fresh and composed.

Finally, before concluding each time of sharing, close your eyes and visualize yourself, your spouse and Jesus standing together with your arms around one another's shoulders. Spend several minutes visualizing this scene. You may wish to imagine the resented person verbally accepting what you have said to him/her. In actuality your part-

---

Emptying the container of resentment is only half the battle. You need to fill that void with feelings and expressions of love, acceptance, forgiveness and friendship.

---

ner may *not* accept what you say and could instead become angry. What is important is that *you* have taken these steps to release your resentment.

As you may have realized by now, an exercise like this, directed toward your spouse, may uncover other existing hurts from relationships with parents or others in your past. You may need to follow these steps of writing and verbalizing your resentments with others in mind. In fact, forgiving your spouse may hinge on forgiving others in your past. Repeat this exercise as often as necessary to clear your memory of bad feelings.

Another helpful method for releasing resentment is to write a letter to the offending person. However, this letter is never to be delivered. It is a tool for you to express your resentful feelings in a more personal and detailed fashion than a list.

Start your letter as you would any other letter: Dear_____.
But in this letter you need not concern yourself with style, neatness or

proper grammar and punctuation. Concentrate on identifying, releasing and expressing your feelings on paper in great detail.

You may find it difficult to get going, but as you press on you will sense your feelings and words beginning to flow out. Don't hold back! Let out all the bad feelings that have been churning inside you. Don't stop to evaluate whether the feelings you express are good or bad, right or wrong. The feelings are there and need to be expressed. If you find the process emotionally exhausting, you may want to complete it in stages over several days.

I ask many of my clients in therapy to write such a letter at home and bring it to their next session. Often they hand me the letter as they enter the room. "No," I say. "I'd like you to keep the letter and we will use it later." At the appropriate time I ask them to read the letter aloud to an empty chair in the room, imagining that the resented person is there listening.

I remember one client who wrote a very extensive letter to her mother. She was surprised when I asked her to read it in my presence. During the first 15 minutes of reading my client was very broken and tearful. But through the last five minutes, the weeping ceased and there was a positive, bright lilt to her voice as she concluded her letter. Some very painful issues of her past were successfully dealt with through the exercise of writing and reading a letter.

Give a Positive Response

There is one final step that is a very necessary part of releasing resentment. Not only is it important to express and give up feelings of resentment, it is also essential that you project a positive response to the individual who has wronged you. Emptying the container of resentment is only half the battle. You need to fill that void with feelings and expressions of love, acceptance, forgiveness and friendship.

I have had a number of clients state that they have neither positive nor negative feelings toward some individuals. They are blasé. But what they have really developed is a state of emotional insulation toward certain persons. And insulation usually means a blockage of some sort. Neutrality must be replaced by positive, productive feelings.

The exercise of developing a positive response to resented individuals is a means of finding any last vestiges of resentment and eliminating them. Take a blank sheet of paper and write your spouse's full name (or the name of the resented person) at the top. Below the name write a salutation as in a letter: Dear_____.

Under the salutation write, "I forgive you for...." Then complete the sentence by writing down everything that has bothered you over the years. For example, someone may write, "I forgive you for always trying to control my life."

Next, stop to capture the immediate thought that comes to mind after writing the statement of forgiveness. Does the thought contradict the concept of forgiveness you have just expressed? Do you feel an inner rebuttal or protest of some kind? Is there any anger, doubt, or caustic feeling that runs against your desire to forgive? Write all these contradictory thoughts immediately below your "I forgive you for..." statement. Don't be surprised if your thoughts are so firm or vehement that it seems like you have not done any forgiving at all. Continue the exercise by writing "I forgive you for..." statements, followed by your immediate thoughts, even if they are contradictory.

Keep repeating the process until you have drained all the pockets of resistance and resentment. You will know you have reached that point when you can think of no more contradictions or resentful responses to the statement of forgiveness you have written. Some people finish this exercise with only a few contradictory responses. Others have a great deal of resentment and use several pages to record their feelings.

The following is a typical example of how a husband forgave his wife for her coldness toward him and her extramarital affair. Notice how his protests and contradictions to forgiveness become progressively less intense. Finally his resentment drains away to the place where he can simply say, "I forgive you," and feel no further need for rebuttal.

Dear Liz, I forgive you for the way you've treated me over the years and for your unfaithfulness.
I'm just saying that. I can't forgive you right now. I'm so hurt.

Dear Liz, I forgive you for...
I'm hurt and angry. I've put up with you for years.

Dear Liz, I forgive you for...
How do I know I can trust you after what you did?

Dear Liz, I forgive you for...
How do I know you're going to be any different? I can't take your coldness any more.

Dear Liz, I forgive you for...
I'm really hesitant to open myself up to you any more.

Dear Liz, I forgive you for...
I do love you, but I've been rejected so much. I'm afraid of being rejected again.

Dear Liz, I forgive you for...
I would like to forgive you at times. I don't like these feelings I have.

Dear Liz, I forgive you for...
It's a bit better as I write this. I feel a bit funny and awkward as I do this.

Dear Liz, I forgive you for...
I wish this had never happened.

Dear Liz, I forgive you for...
I know I've blamed you and I feel you're responsible. But maybe I contributed to the problems in some way.

Dear Liz, I forgive you for...
My anger is less and maybe someday it will go away.

Dear Liz, I forgive you for...

Jim wrote this letter to Liz one day, then three days later he repeated the exercise. In his second letter, after writing eight contradictory thoughts, Jim was able to conclude with several "I forgive you..." statements with no rebuttals.

After completing your own version of this exercise, sit opposite an empty chair as described earlier. Visualize the resented person sitting in the empty chair verbally accepting your forgiveness. Take as long as you need for this step because it is very important. When you have finished the exercise destroy your list of statements, without showing it to anyone, as a symbol that, "Old things are passed away; behold, all things are become new" (2 Cor. 5:17, *KJV*).

Forgive, Forget and Be Free

Holding resentment toward your spouse will keep you living in the past, contaminate the present and limit the possibilities of the future. As Lloyd Ogilvie says:

> The sure sign that we have an authentic relationship with God is that we believe more in the future than in the past. The past can be neither a source of confidence nor a condemnation. God graciously divided our life into days and years so that we could let go of yesterdays and anticipate our tomorrows. For the past mistakes, He offers forgiveness and an ability to forget. For our tomorrows, He gives us the gift of expectation and excitement.[3]

One of our problems is that most of us have a better memory than God does. We cling to our past hurts and nurse them, and in so doing

*If you do not only love
forgive an enemy
are you not just
like unbelievers...*

Ridding Your Romance of Resentment   115

we experience difficulty in the present with our partner. We are actually attempting to pull rank on God when we refuse to forgive our spouse or ourselves—something He has already done. Our lack of forgiveness not only fractures our relationship with others but with God as well.

Lewis Smedes offers a helpful insight:

> Is it fair to be stuck to a painful past? Is it fair to be walloped again and again by the same old hurt? Vengeance is having a videotape planted in your soul that cannot be turned off. It plays the painful scene over and over again inside your mind. It hooks you into its instant replays. And each time it replays, you feel the clap of pain again. Is it fair?
>
> Forgiving turns off the videotape of pained memory. Forgiving sets you free. Forgiving is the only way to stop the cycle of unfair pain turning in your memory.[4]

Can you accept your spouse for what he or she is, whatever that person may have done? Acceptance means forgiving to the point that you no longer allow what has occurred in the past to influence you anymore. Only through complete acceptance can you be free—free to develop yourself, to experience life, to communicate openly, to love yourself and your spouse entirely.

Lloyd Ogilvie asks the question:

> Who's your burden? Whom do you carry emotionally, in memory, or in conscience? Who causes you difficult reactions of guilt, fear, frustrations, or anger? That person belongs to God. He's carrying him or her too, you know! Isn't it about time to take the load off, face the unresolved dynamics of the relationship and forgive and forget?[5]

Forgiveness means saying, "It is all right; it is over. I no longer resent you nor see you as an enemy. I love you even if you cannot love me in return." When you refuse to forgive, you inflict inner torment upon yourself, and that makes you miserable and ineffective. But when you forgive someone for hurting you, you perform spiritual surgery on your soul. You cut away the wrong that was done to you. You see your "enemy" through the magic eyes that can heal your soul. Separate the person from the hurt and let the hurt go the way children open their hands and let a trapped butterfly go free.

Then invite that person back into your mind, fresh, as if a piece of history between you has been erased, its grip on your memory broken. Reverse the seemingly irreversible flow of pain within you.[6]

We are only able to forgive because God has forgiven us. He has given us a beautiful model of forgiveness in Christ's redemptive sacrifice. Allowing God's forgiveness to permeate our lives and renew us is the first step toward wholeness. And the eradication of the barrier of resentment allows intimacy and romance to bloom!

Notes

1. Lewis B. Smedes, "Forgiveness: The Power to Change the Past," *Christianity Today* (January 7, 1983), p. 26.
2. The approach described in relinquishing resentments and forgiving others is used, in varying forms, by many therapists and ministers including the following: Matthew L. Linn and D. Linn, *Healing of Memories* (Ramsey, NJ: Paulist Press, 1974), see pp. 94-96; Dennis and Matthew Linn, *Healing Life's Hurts* (Ramsey, NJ: Paulist Press, 1977), see pp. 218ff; Howard Halpern, *Cutting Loose: A Guide to Adult Terms with Your Parents* (New York: Bantam, 1978), see pp. 212ff. (The empty chair technique described in Gestalt literature is described in this section); David L. Luecke, *The Relationship Manual* (Columbia, MD: Relationship Institute, 1981), see pp. 88-91; see also past issues of *The Journal of Christian Healing*, published by the Institute of Christian Healing, 103 Dudley Avenue, Narbelk, PA 19072.
3. Lloyd John Ogilvie, *God's Best for My Life* (Eugene, OR: Harvest House, 1981), p. 1.
4. Smedes, "Forgiveness: The Power to Change the Past," p. 26.
5. Ogilvie, *God's Best for My Life*, p. 9.
6. Lewis B. Smedes, *Forgive and Forget* (San Francisco: Harper and Row, Publishers, Inc., 1984), p. 37.

SEVEN

Prospering in the Midst of a Love Recession

*C*urrently, our country is experiencing an economic recession and many Americans are severely affected. Some people have had to make major economic and career adjustments; some may even go bankrupt and have to start over financially. The attitudes of different individuals have much to do with how they handle the financial setbacks of the recession. Some are devastated emotionally since they had never anticipated that financial ruin could fall upon them. Others feel that the Lord has let them down. They assume that being a Christian automatically guarantees economic stability.

Have you ever experienced a love recession in your marriage? Some of you know what I'm talking about, but others may be a bit threatened by what I'm going to say. There are times when marital love is intense, strong and vibrant. But there are also times when you begin to question your love for your spouse or your spouse's love for you. For some reason love recedes from a previously higher and more fulfilling level. Sometimes this occurs at predictable stages in marriage, such as honeymoon, childbearing, empty nest, etc. It can happen after two years of marriage, or 20 years, or 40 years. Yes, just like a financial recession, a love recession can even happen to Christians who think their marriage will only climb upward.

When people feel that their love (or their partner's love) is weakening, they experience a multitude of feelings. A love recession can be frightening, frustrating and even depressing. Anxiety rises and you look for an answer. It can be threatening for a couple to face up to a sense of diminishing love, but it can also become a time of positive growth. It is like a financial crisis in which the way you respond can have a large bearing on your survival. Unlike the victim of a financial recession, however, you are never bankrupt of currency in a love recession. You never run out of love. You just need to look for it in some new places so you can grow and develop new love in your relationship.

Think about the following questions and jot down your answers:

Have you ever experienced a love recession at any time in your marriage? If so, what do you think contributed to it?

Are you experiencing a love recession at this time in your marriage?

Has your spouse ever experienced a love recession? If so, what do you think contributed to it?

Have you ever discussed your periods of receding love with your spouse? If not, what keeps you from doing so?

What would you do if a love recession happened to you? Consider the following and choose what you might do:

1. Accept the love recession as normal.
2. Become upset and frantic.
3. Get in touch with my feelings and begin to discover the reasons.
4. Think of a love recession as an indication for positive growth and change.
5. Consider developing some new positive responses toward my spouse.
6. Consider the content of my thought life toward my spouse.

You may be thinking that your love has been the same throughout the duration of your marriage and you have never really experienced a love recession. Let's take a look at your love history. Complete the following love recession chart. You may find that both of you have experienced love "highs" and love "lows" throughout your marriage. The points of your partner's highs and lows may not coincide with yours. Don't worry—it's normal.

Often a love recession occurs when couples move from one stage of marriage to another (e.g., childlessness to parenting) or when they go through one of the transitions of life (30s, mid-life, etc.). You feel

Super love							
High love							
Strong love							
Average love							
Low love							
No love							
	First Met	Court-ship Yrs.	0-5 Yrs.	5-10 Yrs.	10-15 Yrs.	15-20 Yrs.	20+

alone or isolated, and think that something is wrong with you. You begin questioning whether you ever loved your partner in the first place and wondering if the diminished love can ever become strong again. No, you are not the only person who has ever experienced this phenomenon. Don't panic. And don't ignore what is happening. One

---

If and when a love recession hits, accept what you are experiencing and feeling as something that is quite normal.

---

of the unhealthiest ways to respond is to ignore or deny what is occurring. These experiences and feelings happen to many couples. It is important to remember that, with honest acceptance of the situation and some positive action, your love can and will increase.

But what do you tend to do when your love is in a recession? Respond to each option below on a scale of 0-10 (0 means not at all and 10 means very much so).

When my love is in a recession, I would like...

More romance

0   1   2   3   4   5   6   7   8   9   10

More variety in my life

0   1   2   3   4   5   6   7   8   9   10

More space

0   1   2   3   4   5   6   7   8   9   10

Someone to help me talk through it

0   1   2   3   4   5   6   7   8   9   10

More closeness

0   1   2   3   4   5   6   7   8   9   10

To give more love

0   1   2   3   4   5   6   7   8   9   10

To get more love

0   1   2   3   4   5   6   7   8   9   10

To feel special and appreciated

0   1   2   3   4   5   6   7   8   9   10

To evaluate what I want in this marriage

0   1   2   3   4   5   6   7   8   9   10

Some time away with my spouse to work on our relationship

0   1   2   3   4   5   6   7   8   9   10

So what can you do when a love recession hits? For that matter, what can you do to minimize the occurrences of recession? Good questions. The rest of the chapter is devoted to supplying you with some helpful, practical answers. If you are presently experiencing a love recession, or want to equip yourself for handling recession in the future, let me suggest two additional resources. My book, *How to Speak Your Spouse's Language* (Revell), focuses on the importance of communication in all types of relationships, including marriage. The book will be a helpful follow-up to the topic of chapter 8—learning to speak your spouse's love language. If you have a resistive or non-responsive partner, and you are becoming weary of trying to help that person respond, I recommend my book, *How to Have a Creative Crisis* (Word).

The second half of the book is devoted to the topic of creating a positive, controlled crisis in order to bring about change in a relationship.

When Recession Happens

You can allow a love recession to devastate you or you can respond to it as a time of growth and change. If and when a love recession hits, accept what you are experiencing and feeling as something that is quite normal. Don't deny your feelings. Instead, write them down—both positive and negative. Set up a convenient appointment to communicate your feelings. Then lovingly share the entire range of your thoughts and feelings with your partner, not as an ultimatum for him/her to change but as a point of information signalling your interest in making your marriage stronger.

Evaluate your thought life toward yourself and your partner over recent months. Evaluate your behavior and your partner's behavior over that time and be sure you give yourselves credit for the positives. We all have a tendency to focus on defects, failures and negatives rather than on the positives, even though the positives often outweigh the negatives. When our perspective is out of balance it often leads us to talk ourselves out of being in love with our partners!

Consciously try some new loving behaviors toward your partner. Make a special effort to act out your love even if the feelings of love are not as strong as they once were. Consider the various ways of expressing your love to your partner that are suggested in this book.

Let's consider some steps you can take to build and enhance the love in your marriage. The initial step is to identify the termites that might be weakening the structure. The termites in a marriage, like resentment in chapter 6, subtly and steadily eat away at the foundation of a relationship. Some other termites endangering a marriage include excessive attention to hobbies, over-extending oneself in work and television. Yes, television! As Lois Wyse points out in the following poem, television has the potential for causing problems in a marriage.

Television.
So many television marriages.
How do we avoid a television marriage,
That playing out of lives against the background of the tube?
Instead of our two lives filling the room,
There are their two lives and the eleven o'clock news with
Constant commercial interruptions.
Instead of what you say and what I say,
It is what Dick and Johnny and their guests say.
You don't laugh with me;
I don't laugh with you.
All the wit comes pouring out of the tube,
And we laugh at it together.
The more we avoid talking,
The more passive the relationship becomes.
Television permits us to walk through life
With minor speaking parts.
There is so much talk coming at us all day and all night
That we sit in quiet relief because we do not have to speak.
And the more we fail to speak,
The more difficult speaking becomes.
We push everything deeper and deeper into
Some small, dark part of ourselves.
We stuff it deeper and deeper and deeper.
It becomes so hard and deep we forget it until
It comes back to haunt us in our dreams the nights we sleep
And in our turning-tossing wakefulness the nights we don't.

We treat our love with diffidence.
We are afraid to say the three most important love words of all:
      I need you.
Only those needs that can be expressed can be answered,
And of all human needs,
The greatest is love.

I need you.
I need you.
There, I said it.
Turn off the tube, please.
I need you.
I need us.[1]

Take a few minutes and list what you think are some of the present or potential termites that could bring about a love recession in your marriage. Then list some from your spouse's perspective. After you have both completed the exercise, talk together about your lists.

TERMITES IN OUR MARRIAGE

From my perspective	From spouse's perspective

Reach Out and Touch

Now that we have identified some possible hindrances to love, let's look at some of the ways to keep love alive. One very practical way is through touching. I'm not talking here about erotic sexual caressing and fondling that leads into the bedroom. Rather I am referring to daily acts of physical contact that are ends of romance, love and communication in themselves.

Don't get me wrong—I'm in favor of sexual touching in marriage. But there is much more to romantic touching than that which leads to the bedroom. Over the years I have heard hundreds of women tell why they do not respond to their husbands' touching. It's not because they don't enjoy sex. But as one woman put it (whose comments reflect the feelings of many other women), "When he caresses me, hugs me or strokes my hand, I know what he has in mind. I wish he could give me affection without an ulterior motive. I enjoy sex, but he doesn't realize that the casual touches during the day can lead to greater sex in the bedroom!" Very well stated.

Physical contact in marriage is essential to building intimacy and enhancing the act of lovemaking. Spouses affectionately touching one another generate the sensations of warmth, security and emotional satisfaction that every human being craves. Patting, stroking and caressing carry a nonverbal message of endearment and tenderness that we have all needed since childhood. And that physical need does not leave us when we grow to adulthood.

No amount of cultural restriction or stereotyping can eliminate this need for physical contact, although Americans tend to be less "touchy" in relationships than other cultures. Travel to Europe, Africa or Asia and you might be surprised to find how adults hug, hold hands and lean against one another. In the book *The Gift of Touch* (Putnam Publishing Group), author Helen Colton cites the observations of a social scientist who contrasted the touching habits of Americans with those of the French. In an hour's time the French friends touched each other about 100 times while the Americans touched no more than 3 or 4 times.

How high is your level of need for being touched? Use the chart below to express your need and your spouse's need.

Indicate the intensity of your need for touching by circling the appropriate number (0 means no need, 5 means moderate need, 10 means great need). Do the same for your spouse on the second chart.

My need for touching

0 1 2 3 4 5 6 7 8 9 10

My spouse's need for touching

0 1 2 3 4 5 6 7 8 9 10

Touching is an expression of affection. Women tend to desire affectionate touching more than men. A woman's need for physical contact may be seen as a weakness, but it is really a strength. Touching is a plus to all who welcome it. We men could learn much from what our wives already know about closeness.

The importance of warmth, tenderness and caring is powerfully portrayed by Donna Swanson in "Minnie Remembers."

How long has it been since someone touched me? Twenty years I've been a widow. Respected. Smiled at. But never touched...Oh God, I'm so lonely. I remember Hank and the babies. How else can I remember them but together? Hank didn't seem to mind if my body thickened and faded a little. He loved it and he loved to touch it. And the children hugged me, a lot...Oh God, I'm lonely! God, why didn't we raise the kids to be silly and affectionate as well as dignified and proper? They drive up in their fine cars. They come to my room to pay their respects. They chatter brightly and reminisce. But they don't touch me. They call me Mom, or Mother, or Grandma. Never Minnie. My mother called me Minnie. So did my friends. Hank called me Minnie, too. But they're gone. And so is Minnie.[2]

Have You Hugged Your Spouse Today?

Hugging is an important element of touching. And hugging is a vital expression of love. I know. I went for 15 years without receiving a hug from our son Matthew. It wasn't that he held back or didn't care. He wasn't capable. Matthew was a profoundly mentally retarded boy who died at the age of 22 and had the mental ability of about an 18-month-old. He lived in our home until he was 11 and then moved to Salem Christian Home in Ontario, California.

For years Joyce and I affectionately reached out to Matthew with hugs and kisses, but he did not respond. Through this process we learned to give love without receiving love in return. And we accepted Matthew's limitation even though we eagerly looked forward to the time when we might receive a hug from him.

Then one day we wrapped our arms around Matthew and, for the first time, felt his arms reaching around us and squeezing. It is hard to describe how precious Matthew's hug was to us after having lived without it for so many years. After that first hug there were several other times when Matthew would respond with his simple embrace. And sometimes we held out our arms and said, "Matthew, hug," and he reached to give us a hug. Please—never take the expression of a hug for granted.

Do you know that your body chemistry actually changes when you are physically close to another person? If you learned from your childhood to fear physical closeness, your body will respond to touching with adrenaline, as though a person drawing near was a threat. But if you learned the delight of physical closeness as a child through cuddling and hugging, your body will respond with feelings of well-being, security and relaxation.

How would you respond to a doctor who prescribed that you receive four hugs a day? Physical hugging is very therapeutic. Hugging can lift depression and breathe new life into a tired body. When you are touched the amount of hemoglobin in your body increases significantly. The surge of hemoglobin tones up the whole body, helps prevent disease and speeds recovery from illness.[3]

Do you hug your spouse and others? Do you receive hugs? One of my favorite quotes is, "Every marriage needs to be picked up and hugged and given personal attention."[4] Hugging is a significant preventative and cure for love recession.

Putting in a Good Word

Another way to keep love alive and fight recession is to bless your spouse. The word "blessing" in the New Testament is based on two

---

When you seek to learn your partner's wishes in order to meet them as best you can, you are implementing the model of servanthood as portrayed in Scripture.

Greek words that mean "well" and "word." Blessing your spouse literally means to speak well of that person.

You can bless your partner by what you say to him/her and how you say it. You should speak lovingly and encouragingly in order to make your mate's life better and fuller, not out of a sense of duty. Sincere compliments, words of encouragement and "sweet somethings" thoughtfully spoken are romance builders and love enrichers. Also your verbal response to your partner's words is important. Saying thank you, expressing appreciation and offering requested information or opinions with kindness will bless your mate. Perhaps the ultimate way of verbally blessing your partner is to lift that person to the Lord in prayer and intervene on his/her behalf.[5] Verbal expressions of gratitude and affirmation cannot be overstressed.

There is another biblical approach to keeping love alive that parallels blessing—and that is edifying. To edify means to build up another (see Rom. 14:19; 15:2; 1 Thess. 5:11). You can edify your spouse by becoming his/her greatest fan. You are in the front row of the grandstand for your partner's every endeavor cheering, "Go for it! You can do it! I believe in you!" You are the president of your spouse's fan club encouraging, "You have the capability, value and worth regardless of the task. I'm praying for you."

As you edify your spouse in this way you will increase his/her sense of self-worth. The result will be an increase in your spouse's capacity to give of himself/herself to you in love.

I like the ways Dr. Ed Wheat suggests for building up partners:

1. Make a decision to never again be critical of your partner in thought, word and deed. This should be a decision backed up by action until it becomes a habit that you would not change even if you could.

2. Spend time studying your spouse so you develop a sensitivity to the areas in which the person feels a lack. Discover creative ways to build your spouse up in those weak areas.

3. Spend time thinking daily of positive qualities and behavior patterns you admire and appreciate in your spouse. Make a list and thank God for these.

4. Consistently verbalize praise and appreciation and do this in a specific and generous manner.

5. Recognize what your spouse does, but also who your spouse is. Let him or her know that you respect them for what they accomplish.

6. Husbands, publicly and privately show your wife how special she is to you. Keep your attention focused on your wife and not on other women.

7. Wives, show your husband how important he is in your life. Ask his opinion and value his judgments.

8. Respond to each other physically and facially. Our faces are the most distinctive and expressive parts of us. Smile with your

total face. Your spouse needs to receive more of your smiles than others.

9. Be courteous to each other in private and in public. Each of you should be a VIP in your home.[6]

How Can I Love You?

I have talked with many couples who feel that they have tried to demonstrate love and meet the needs of their spouses but keep missing the mark. To eliminate misunderstanding and mind reading, it is far better to share with one another your needs, wants and desires in a specific yet nondemanding manner. When you seek to learn your partner's wishes in order to meet them as best you can, you are implementing the model of servanthood as portrayed in the Scripture.

One of the most effective ways of meeting each other's love needs and wants is to launch into the "Cherishing Days" exercise. Sound interesting? It can be very interesting and it is easy to implement. Each partner makes a list of small cherishing behaviors that he or she would enjoy receiving from the other. These requested behaviors should have four characteristics:

1. They must be specific and positive. For example, Janice would like Jim to sit next to her on the couch as they watch the news after dinner. Janice has made a positive request for a desired behavior instead of complaining, "You ignore me and are preoccupied with the TV."
2. The small cherishing behaviors must not be concerned with past conflicts or old demands.
3. The positive behaviors must be such that they can be accomplished on an everyday basis.
4. The behaviors must be achievable—they do not require excessive time or expense.

Take several days to compile your lists. Think back to the most satisfying times of your courtship and marriage to discover ideas for your list. Some of the behaviors you think of may seem trivial or somewhat embarrassing to you. It's perfectly all right. Include them on your list as long as they reflect valid personal wants or needs.

Once your list of 15 to 20 cherishing behaviors is completed, exchange lists with your partner and discuss the cherishing behaviors you are requesting from each other. Be sure to tell your spouse *how* you would like each behavior performed for you. For example, if you request a back rub at bedtime, specify light skin rub or deep muscle massage, with lotion or without, etc. As you discuss your written behaviors, feel free to add others to the list as you think of them.

After your discussion declare the next seven days to be "Cherishing Days." Make a commitment to put your partner's list into practice. Try to accomplish as many of the cherishing behaviors on the list as possible each day. Focus your attention and energies on what you do for your spouse, not what he/she does for you. At the end of seven days you may evaluate whether you will continue the exercise for another week.

Why does this work so well to encourage love and romance? Because the list of positive behaviors that you exchange consists of requested, discussed and agreed upon acts of love. The guesswork of "What shall I do for him/her? Will he/she like it?" is eliminated. Also, the commitment is short term—you are only responsible for seven days. And the behaviors are purposely simple and easily achievable. The margin of failure is greatly reduced.

Another important factor in the success of this exercise is the commitment of each individual to the "I must change first" principle. You are not keeping score of your spouse's efforts. You are too busy concentrating on accomplishing his/her list. And with each behavior comes a positive response, which encourages the giver to continue. As each person gives and receives positive loving acts, the bond of love will grow stronger.

Most couples decide to continue the exercise after completing the seven-day commitment. They find that the positives of filling each other's wants and needs eliminate the negatives of love-recessive behavior patterns. The "Cherishing Days" exercise is a practical, simple application of scriptural admonitions to kindness, love, edification, etc.

Here is a sample list of cherishing behaviors that many people have found helpful:

1. Greet me with a hug and kiss before we get out of bed in the morning.
2. When you're out walking, bring back a flower or a leaf.
3. Look at me and smile.
4. Call me during the day and tell me something pleasant.
5. Turn off the lights and light a candle when we have dinner.
6. Put on a favorite record and come sit next to me and hold my hand.
7. Ask me how I spent my day.
8. Wash my back in the tub or shower.
9. Pick me up at work or at the bus stop as a surprise.
10. Put a surprise love note in my lunch or article of clothing.
11. Tell me how much you enjoy having breakfast with me.
12. Tell the children (in front of me) that I'm a good parent.
13. When we sit together, put your arm around me.
14. Have coffee with me in the morning before we wake the children so we can have a five-minute talk together.
15. Date me and make all the arrangements.
16. Hold me at night before we go to sleep.
17. Ask my opinion about world affairs or the sermon at church.
18. Hug me and say you love me for no special reason.
19. Greet me with a smile when we first see each other at the end of the day.
20. Use endearing words with me sometime.
21. When we are out, wink or blow a kiss to me.[7]

This list is just a sample. I'm sure you can add to the list ideas of your own. Create your own list of behaviors that are important to you.

How About a Date?

Notice that one of the items on the sample list is dating. Dating is vital in the process of courtship and perhaps even more important in marriage as an antidote to love recession.

Quite often as I work with couples in counseling I encourage them to date one another. "Where do we go on a date?" they ask. "How do I know what he or she would like to do on a date?" The first step in answering these questions is to conduct a date interview. When your spouse is in a relaxed mood or when the two of you are out to dinner, say, "I need ten minutes of your time to conduct an interview with you. I can't tell you what it is for at this time, but you will eventually know more about it." Then ask your spouse the following questions:

1. When you used to date in high school or college, what were your favorite types of dates? Why?
2. During those years, did you dream about an outstanding date that you always wanted to have but never did? (I don't mean with a certain movie star!)
3. What are your favorite colors?
4. What is your favorite type of music?
5. What are your favorite travel spots to visit?
6. What are your favorite foods?
7. What type of restaurant do you like best?
8. What are your three favorite desserts?
9. What are your favorite flowers?
10. What is your favorite cologne/perfume?
11. What are your favorite types of books?
12. What shows or plays do you enjoy the most and why?
13. What three types of activities would you like to try, given a chance to do so?

The results of the interview should give you ample ideas for numerous dates, either simple or extravagant, that incorporate many of your partner's "favorites."

Three Little Words

Saying "I love you" is a message that needs to be conveyed to your spouse every day. But creativity helps you convey the message in many ways that show you really mean it. So here are some wild and zany ways to get your loving message across. Yes, you may feel a little silly or embarrassed trying some of these at first. But the response is well worth the effort:

1. Find books on other languages in the library or a bookstore and copy "I love you" in several languages. Either write out the message or learn how to pronounce the message properly.
2. Write the words "I love you" backwards and place the message in your spouse's shoe.
3. When you steam up the bathroom, write "I love you" on the mirror and ask your spouse to come in while it's still readable. (You might also consider taking a shower together!)
4. Put a balloon in the car with the words "I love you" on it or in it.
5. Spell "I love you" with candies on your spouse's pillow, desk, favorite chair, etc.
6. Make a huge "I love you" banner and tape it to the ceiling over your bed.
7. Carve "I love you" in wood and float your message in the fish tank, orange juice container or even the toilet!
8. Paint "I love you" on a household object (refrigerator, mirror, garage door, etc.) with removable paint.
9. Buy an inexpensive glider and soar it toward your spouse pulling a tiny "I love you" banner (or paint "I love you" on the wings).
10. Take your spouse kite flying. Make sure your kite says "I love

you" in some creative way. (The new kites are great! My wife and I took up kite flying last year.)

11. Bake the message on or inside a pastry (cake, fortune cookie, etc.). Or put a written "I love you" message inside the Thanksgiving or Christmas turkey. Imagine your spouse's reaction as he/she unfolds the message in front of your guests!

12. If you have a friend with a talking bird (parrot, mynah, cockatiel), see if the bird can be taught to say "I love you," adding your spouse's name. (Be sure the bird doesn't have an obscene vocabulary as well!)

13. For a special occasion, write "I love you" on your eyelids so the message shows when you close your eyes.

14. If you have a telephone answering recorder leave an "I love you" message on it for your spouse.

15. Bury or hide the message and give your spouse a treasure map to find it. It is also nice to have a small gift with the message since the searching entails some time and effort.

16. Say "I love you" in sign language. Simply raise your right hand palm forward, lifting thumb, index finger and pinkie while keeping the two middle fingers folded down.

17. If you have a swimming pool, write "I love you" on the bottom of the pool with different objects.

18. Write "I love you" on the kitchen counter with sugar or flour.

19. If your spouse keeps a daily calendar, write "I love you" messages on several of the dates.

20. Write "I love you" very small and fasten it inside your spouse's glasses or sunglasses with clear tape.

21. Tie the message to one of your pets in such a way that your spouse will have to take it off the pet to read it.

22. Record "I love you" messages on audio- or video-cassette tape and mail it to your spouse. Write a wild title on the tape's label.

23. Give your spouse an "I love you" ornament for Christmas.

24. Purchase a dozen Valentine's cards in February and send one to your spouse each month of the year.

25. Buy a package of candy and open it carefully at one of the seams. Put several love messages inside with your spouse's name on them, then reseal the package. Make sure your spouse is the one to open the candy—not the kids!

26. Purchase a book of blank pages at a stationery store. Write a love message inside using one word per page. (Be creative since the book may contain 50-100 pages.) Take the book to your public library, tell the librarian your plan and ask him/her to keep the book for you until your spouse comes to claim it. Send your spouse a card (perhaps a reserve book card purchased from the library) with a message that the library is holding a special reserved book for him/her. (How wild can you get!)

27. Get ideas for handmade love message cards from stationery or card stores. Be creative with size, color, design, etc.

28. Place an "I love you" message in the "personals" column of the local newspaper. Send your spouse an "anonymous" message to read the personals every day that week until the message is discovered.

29. Write each word from the message "I love you" on three separate sheets of paper and put each in an envelope. Ask three different friends to drop off one envelope to your spouse during the week.

30. Now *you* can be creative. List four other ways to say "I love you" that might be special for your spouse:

Many men and women enjoy receiving special love notes or letters. There are many creative ways to vary your notes to keep them fresh and romantic. Here are a number of suggestions that have worked well for other lovers:

1. Hide a note in a pocket or some special place where your spouse will be sure to find it during the day.
2. If you are going to be away from your spouse for several days, purchase several cards in advance and mail one each day. You may want to leave each day's love message incomplete with the line, "To be continued." Continue the message on the next card. (On two occasions I have been in the back woods of Alaska and Canada with no access to the postal system. I simply left my prearranged cards with a friend who mailed them on the appropriate days.)
3. Twice my wife has placed a heart or romantic sticker on my racquetball equipment without telling me. In the locker room I received comments or curious glances from the other men, which puzzled me until I realized I was the last to discover my wife's hidden love messages.
4. Send a personal note or card to your spouse's place of employment. Variations include a telegram, helium balloon, flowers, or UPS package delivered to your spouse's desk.
5. Leave a large musical eighth note, cut out of black construction paper, on the car windshield with the title of an appropriate love song written on it.
6. Send a love note with each letter on a separate slip of paper so your spouse must piece the letters together to figure out the message.

Did you know that former president Harry Truman was a dyed-in-the-wool romantic? He pursued his wife Bess for many years before she agreed to marry him. He first asked her in 1911 and they were finally married in 1919. But once he married her, Mr. Truman continued to romance his wife. When he was away from her he wrote love letters. And when Bess Truman died in the early 1980s, more than 1,200 letters from her husband were discovered in her home. Harry never stopped courting Bess.

Did you write any love letters to each other when you were courting? If so, did you save any? Find them and enjoy an evening together reading old love letters to each other. You can still write love letters too. Spend some time creating your letter and then inscribe it on some kind of special paper. Perhaps you could send it to your spouse's work place, but be sure to mark it "Personal." Or you could hand deliver it to your spouse in a romantic setting.

Here is a portion of a touching love letter written by Ingrid Trobisch to her husband, Walter, who introduces the excerpt:

> Ingrid and I know what the risk of loving means. We were separated by continents when we were engaged; she as a missionary teacher in Cameroun and I as a pastor in a large congregation in West Germany. Let me share what she wrote to me from her lonely station:
>
> "I want to tell you why I love you. When I picture you in my mind, I can see you stretching out your hand to me. I trust your hand for it is the hand of a safe and secure man. It is true, you walk a little ahead of me, but when you realize I'm getting out of breath and can't quite keep up, you stand still. You turn around and give me your hand to help me over hard places. Then I come very near to you and you talk to me and comfort me. You don't make fun of my thoughts, neither are you threatened by them if they challenge you to try a new path.
>
> "When I am weak and need protection, I know that you are stronger than I, and so I take hold of your hand because I know that you will never use your strength to make me feel inferior.
>
> "But you need me too and you are not ashamed to show it. Even though you are strong and manly, you can also be helpless as a child. Your strong hand can then become an open, empty hand. And I know no greater happiness than to fill it."[8]

Notes

1. "Lovetalk" by Lois Wyse from LOVETALK. Copyright © 1973 by Lois Wyse. Reprinted by permission of Doubleday and Company, Inc., pp. 39-40.
2. "Minnie Remembers," Donna Swanson, *Mind Song* (Nashville: Upper Room, 1978).
3. Leo F. Buscaglia, *Loving Each Other* (New York: Random House, Inc., Fawcett Columbine, 1984), pp. 135-146. Used by permission.
4. Source unknown.
5. Ed Wheat, *Love Life* (Grand Rapids, MI: Zondervan Publishing House, 1980), pp. 178-179.
6. Ibid., pp. 190-191.
7. William J. Lederer, *Marital Choices* (New York: W.W. Norton and Co., 1981), pp. 62-63.
8. Walter Trobisch, *All a Man Can Be* (Downers Grove, IL: InterVarsity Press), p. 89. Used by permission.

EIGHT

Learning to Speak Your Spouse's Language

*T*he couple sat in my office trying to explain their difficulties and interrupting each other as they spoke. Each of them had shared their frustration over not feeling loved by the other.

Nancy looked at me and said, "Bob and I have been married for six years now. We were really in love when we married, but I don't know what has happened. I'm afraid I will get to the place where I'll quit trying...."

"I'm concerned about the same thing," Bob interrupted his wife, "but I think Nancy tries too hard at times."

"But somebody has to try," Nancy retorted. "Even when I try to get romantic you don't seem to respond. I turn down the lights and put on a sexy dress, but that doesn't seem to work. I greet you at the door with a kiss and a hug and encourage you to sit down and relax. I talk to you and ask you about your day, but you don't seem interested. And the more you pull away and don't respond, the more I want to get close to you. I want you to know how I feel."

"But that's just it," Bob responded, looking straight at her. "I've been listening to people all day, then I drive home on that crowded, noisy freeway. I need some peace and quiet and space when I get home. Back off a little and let me settle down, then maybe...."

"Thanks for telling me," Nancy said sarcastically, interrupting him. "That's the first I've ever heard that."

At this point I jumped into the conversation. "It appears that you are learning more about how to respond to each other. But before we go

---

One of the most important adjustments any couple must make in marriage is to learn their partner's "language."

---

on, let me share something that may clear up what's been happening these past several years. It's something you should have been told even before you married. And here it is: Each of you married a foreigner." I paused while Bob and Nancy looked at me with surprise. "That's right," I continued, "you each married a foreigner."

Later that day I sat listening to another couple who had been married for 20 years. "Basically, Norm," Jim said, "the bottom line is this: Mary and I have difficulty communicating."

"Jim, I appreciate your ability to pinpoint the problem," I responded. "Now could you give me a few more specifics? Communication problems are fairly broad. What is a problem for one couple may not be a problem for another."

"We talk but we don't understand each other," Jim summarized. "We're on different wave lengths; we have problems seeing eye to eye. I share something with Mary and she can't see what I'm talking about. And when Mary talks she goes into so much detail and gets off track so often she loses me. I wish she'd just get to the point."

"But, Jim," Mary replied, "I want to tell you what I'm feeling and explain what's going on inside me. But you're so impatient when I'm trying to tell you something. Your eyes wander as though you don't care or want to understand."

"Look," Jim returned, "we've been through this before. At times I don't want to get into a discussion with you because it doesn't end. Why isn't that clear to you?"

Again I moved into the discussion. "During your 20 years of marriage, have there been occasions when you *have* been able to understand each other?" They both seemed hesitant to answer. "Let me ask another question," I pressed on. "Are you able to convey your love in such a way that the other person feels your love?"

"Oh, sure," Jim replied.

"No," Mary said.

"What do you mean, 'no'?" Jim exploded.

"I don't feel you love me at times," Mary answered.

"But I tell you I love you and bring you gifts and cards," Jim explained. "I think I show you all the time that I love you."

"But I don't *feel* that you love me," Mary replied.

Again I entered the dialog. "Even though you've been married 20 years, it appears that neither of you is aware that you each married a foreigner." I paused to let the idea sink in.

"You're right!" Jim said finally. "Half the time I don't even understand what she's talking about." And Mary nodded.

Speaking Foreign Languages

I can make the same statement that I made in the previous case studies to every married man and woman I meet: You married a foreigner! You may have married someone of the same race or nationality, but you each were raised in a different culture. You may both use the same English words in communication but, because of your backgrounds, the same words often have different meanings. And you each employ some words that are not a part of your partner's vocabulary. One of the most important adjustments any couple must make in marriage is to learn their partner's "language."

Perhaps the best way to *illustrate* this truth is by relating another counseling experience I had with a young couple about to be married. *Listen* to the dialog and you may gain a *sense* of what I'm saying. Notice that several words in this section are italicized. The reason for this will be given later in the chapter.

I turned the conversation back to the communication between this young couple. "Bill," I said, "you and your family seem to *focus* in well together as you talk, and Jan, you *feel* good about your communication with your mom. Now, what about the two of you together? What will it take for you two to communicate so that you understand each other?"

They looked at each other and then back at me. I waited and then said, "It's something to think about." I turned to Bill and, *speeding up my rate of speech*, asked, "By the way, Bill, are you and I communicating? Do you think we see *eye to eye*? Do we understand each other?"

Bill replied, "Oh, yes. You seem to *see* what I'm talking about, and I am getting the *picture* of this whole discussion of marrying a foreigner. I wonder, though, if I don't need a passport to marry Jan!"

We all laughed, and I turned to Jan and said *softly*, "How do you *feel* about our communication? Does it make sense?"

"Very much so," Jan answered. "You seem to have a *handle* on what I'm *feeling*, and what you say registers. We seem to speak the same language."

"Good," I said. "It's important that we learn not only to speak the same language but also to make sure we mean the same thing with our words. I have run into so many couples who get irritated and upset in their marriages because of such a simple matter as having different definitions for their words. You know, two people can speak Spanish and not mean the same thing. Two people can speak German and not mean the same thing. We're sitting here speaking English and using some of the same words, but we might have different meanings for them. Your experiences in life, your mind-set, what you intend can give meaning to your words. My wife might ask, 'Could we stop at the store for a minute on our way home, Norm? I'll just be a minute.' I might take the word 'minute' literally, but I had better not, because years of experience have taught me we're talking about fifteen to twenty minutes." Jan and Bill grinned and nodded their heads.

"Bill, has Jan ever said to you, 'Bill, could I talk to you for a minute about something?' and you said 'yes,' assuming she meant a minute, but you're still discussing the issue 30 minutes later?" They both looked amazed, and Bill spoke up *quickly*.

"Tuesday night. That very thing happened Tuesday night. Jan wondered why I was getting uptight."

Jan broke in with, "Well, it was important. Did it matter how long it went on? You agreed we needed to talk about it, and I had *felt* that way for some time."

Bill responded, "Oh, no, it was all right. I just figured it'd be short, since you said a minute."

Jan replied with a bit more feeling, "But many times I *feel* you have set a time limit on our conversations. I almost *sense* that you're impatient and want to get to the bottom line. You don't want to hear all my reasons or feelings. In fact, I wish you would share more details with me. I wear a new outfit and ask you how it looks, and all you say is, 'It looks fine.' Can't you tell me any more about how you *feel* about it?"

Bill looked at me and rolled his eyes upward and then turned to Jan and said loudly, "But I said it *looked* fine. What else do you want to hear?"

I interrupted Bill and said, "On a scale of zero to ten, with zero meaning it looks terrible—like it's out of the rag pile—

and ten meaning it's super—it's outstanding—where does the word 'fine' fall?"

Bill said, "Oh, it's somewhere between an eight and a nine."

Jan looked surprised and blurted out, "How would I know that? That's the first I've heard that fine had any meaning at all!"

"This is what I mean," I interrupted, "when I say you need to define your words. Bill, if you couldn't use the word 'fine' and had to give a three-line description of the dress Jan is wearing, what would you say?"

Bill thought a few seconds and then said, "Well, I like it. The color *looks* good. The dress looks like you, and I like some of the *detail* around the waist. It fits well and I like the curves. It just seems to look like you. And the style is *flashy*."

I turned to Jan, "How do you *feel* about Bill's response?"

She smiled. "That really *feels* good. He really seemed to notice, and I *enjoyed* hearing his description."

Bill jumped in and said, "Well, I could do that, but when I'm with some of my other friends and we say fine, we know what we mean."

"I can understand that," I countered. "When you're with them you speak the same language, but when you're with Jan, you need to speak her language. She wants more detail, more description, more adjectives. That's what registers with her. This is a good example of what I mean by speaking the other person's language. Now that we're talking about it, which one of you tends to give more detail when you talk?" I looked back and forth between Bill and Jan and both of them pointed to Jan and laughed.

"I'm the detail person," Jan said. "Quite often Bill asks me to get to the point and give him the bottom line so he understands what I'm talking about. I just want to make sure that he's going to *grasp* what I am sharing. I've always given a lot of details and *feelings,* but sometimes it's as if he doesn't hear my feelings. He ignores them."

Bill replied, "I don't ignore what you are saying. I do *see* what you are getting at, but I don't always know what to do with those feelings. It's not that I always mind the detail, but I wish you would *focus* on the bottom line first, instead of going around the barn several times and then telling me what you're talking about. I like it straightforward and to the point."

I said, "Bill, you want Jan to communicate with you like a newspaper article."

"A newspaper article? How's that?" Bill asked.

"Most newspaper articles are structured like a pyramid," I continued. "The first sentence is a complete summary statement of what is in the article. Next comes a brief paragraph with some of the most significant summary items expanded. The final larger portion of the article will contain the minute details."

"That's it," Bill said. "An approach like that makes sense to me. I can follow what's going on a lot better, and," he turned to Jan, "I would be willing to hear some more of the detail. But I don't think I need to hear as much detail as you enjoy hearing. I don't want a two-line news summary of what you say, but a Reader's Digest condensation would be helpful." They laughed together.

"Bill," I said, "you're asking Jan to condense some of the details a bit and identify the bottom line right at the start. That helps you *focus* on her conversation better. Is that accurate?" He nodded. "That also means, since Jan enjoys detail, that when you share with her, you will give her more detail than you do now." Bill nodded.

"Now, does my statement about marrying a foreigner make more sense to you?" They both smiled and said, "Yes, definitely!"

"Once again let me go back to the question I asked a few minutes ago. Jan and Bill, what is it going to take, in addition to what we have already pointed out, for the two of you to understand each other and no longer be foreigners? What do you *think*, Bill? What do you *feel*, Jan?"[1]

Did you notice the words in italics in the paragraphs above? Did you figure out why I italicized those words? What *spoke* to you in the interaction? Did you *see* something new about communication styles? Perhaps you have a better *feel* for why I say that you married a foreigner. In your marriage is one of you a communication condenser and the other an amplifier? How does your partner's style affect you? Summarize your response to these questions in the space below:

Language School

The foundation for the expression of love and the blossoming of romance and sexual response in your marriage is this: *Learn to speak one another's language, especially your love language!*

Have you ever approached your spouse with a fantastic idea or dream only to have him/her throw cold water on what you thought was a hot idea? Perhaps it wasn't the idea you suggested but the way you suggested it that drew the "blah" response.

Ralph thought he had a super idea for a romantic, get-away vacation with his wife Elaine. But when he presented it to her, all he got was a negative response. He told me about it at lunch one day. "I don't get it," he said. "Elaine has been wanting us to get away for a romantic time to ourselves. But when I sprang the Mexico trip on her she was about as excited as a duck finding a desert! Boy, did I feel shut down!"

"Tell me how you shared the idea with her," I probed. "I heard you saying you sprang the idea on her."

"Yeah, I did. I rushed through the front door excitedly and said, 'Elaine, look what I have planned for you—a ten-day romantic fling to Mexico!' I waved a brochure in front of her and kept telling her the details. 'Look at the sandy beaches and the quaint little huts. And I hear the fishing is great too. You go out in these little boats so you

---

For effective communication: Present your message so that it matches the way your spouse responds to life and processes information.

---

don't have to fight the crowds. We can bum around the beach barefooted and cook fish over the coals. Isn't that great?'

"Elaine didn't seem interested, and the more I talked it up, the more put out she seemed. I don't understand her. She wants time away from the kids with me, or so she says, and yet she won't take me up on this great idea."

"Does Elaine like surprises," I asked, "or does she enjoy being involved in planning something?"

Ralph thought a moment and then said, "Well, she's quite a planner, you know, and she does have some good ideas. She usually likes to get involved in putting things together."

"Is she a person who can handle a lot of information at one time," I pursued, "or does she prefer to hear the news in smaller pieces so she can think about it and ask questions before making a decision?"

"Boy, it sounds like you've been talking to her!" Ralph sounded surprised. "You hit it on the head. She likes to take things one step at a time. I guess when I came in she felt like she had run into a bull-dozer."

"I know you, Ralph," I continued, "and it sounds to me like you were emphasizing to her the things *you* will enjoy most about the trip—walking on the beach, bouncing around in a small boat, fishing, and eating sooty fish that have been dropped in the coals. Is this Elaine's idea of fun?"

"You're right," Ralph grinned. "Those are some of her least favorite things to do. She likes sight-seeing, shopping, exploring, local history, and art galleries. We can do those on our trip also, but I didn't empha-size them."

"Tell me," I pressed on, "how do you think you could interest Elaine in a trip to Mexico now?"

Ralph thought for a moment. "I would go home and spend some time talking about her day and especially her feelings. At least I've learned that much! Then during dinner I would ask, 'Have you ever dreamed about sleeping where you can hear the gentle waves on the shore at night and eating breakfast on a veranda overlooking those same waves?' Then I'd let her talk about it. Later on I might say, 'Have you ever thought of photographing some Mayan ruins and really get-ting into that ancient time zone?' Knowing Elaine, I think she would then be curious enough to bug me until she squeezed the details out of me. And I think she would be delighted with the idea."

Ralph had learned a significant principle for effective communica-tion: Present your message so that it matches the way your spouse responds to life and processes information. Gear your message to his/her style of communication. Translate your message into his/her language.

Communication Sense

Why are some people so successful at management or sales? Why do some people blend effectively with a wide variety of personality types? Why do some couples get along so well together and really communicate? It's because they understand other people and the way they receive information. We all perceive the world around us by seeing, hearing and feeling. But usually one of these senses is more dominant in each individual. All senses are operational, but each of us tends to respond to life primarily through sight, sound or touch.

A man or woman who understands which sense is dominant in his partner and learns to communicate to that strength will enjoy a closer, loving relationship. That's what I mean by learning to speak each other's love language. Lovers who are more feeling oriented may prefer touching and snuggling over romantic settings or songs. Hearing-oriented people may prefer to converse, listen to soft music and then really get romantic. Seeing-oriented people might prefer gazing at their partner before hugging and snuggling. These preferences are all a part of each individual's love language.

What is your love language? Are you a feeling person? A seeing person? A hearing person? You and your spouse don't need to have the same language, but you do need to learn to speak your partner's love language.

Here is a simple test to help you identify your love language. It is not foolproof, but it can help you and your spouse in love language training. The test will reveal whether you and your mate are seeing, hearing or feeling oriented:

1. Given $1,000 to spend on one of the following, which would you choose?
   a. A new mattress
   b. A new stereo
   c. A new television

   Me_____   Spouse_____

2. Which would you rather do?
   a. Stay home and eat a home-cooked meal
   b. Go out to a concert

c. Go to a movie
   Me_____   Spouse_____

3. Given a choice of activities at a resort, which would you choose?
   a. Going to a lecture
   b. Exploring hiking trails
   c. Relaxing and doing nothing
      Me_____   Spouse_____

4. Which of these rooms would you most enjoy?
   a. One with a terrific view
   b. One with an ocean breeze
   c. One in a quiet corner
      Me_____   Spouse_____

5. To which event would you rather go?
   a. A wedding
   b. An art exhibit
   c. A party with friends
      Me_____   Spouse_____

6. Which are you considered?
   a. Athletic
   b. Intellectual
   c. Humanitarian
      Me_____   Spouse_____

7. How do you most often keep in touch?
   a. By talking on the phone
   b. By writing letters
   c. By having lunch
      Me_____   Spouse_____

8. How do you prefer to spend time?
   a. Talking

    b. Touching

    c. Looking

    Me_____   Spouse_____

9. If you lost your keys, what would you do?

    a. Look for them

    b. Shake your pocketbook or pockets to hear them jingle

    c. Feel around for them

    Me_____   Spouse_____

10. If you were going to be stranded on a desert island, what would you most want to take along?

    a. Some good books

    b. A portable radio

    c. Your sleeping bag

    Me_____   Spouse_____

11. Which type of dresser are you?

    a. Immaculate

    b. Casual

    c. Very casual

    Me_____   Spouse_____

12. Which of these would you rather be?

    a. In the know

    b. Very chic

    c. Comfortable

    Me_____   Spouse_____

13. If you had unlimited money, what would you do?

    a. Buy a great house and stay there

    b. Travel and see the world

    c. Join in the social scene

    Me_____   Spouse_____

14. If you could, which would you rather be?
    a. A great doctor
    b. A great musician
    c. A great painter

    Me_____   Spouse_____

15. Which do you think is sexiest?
    a. Soft lighting
    b. Perfume
    c. Special music

    Me_____   Spouse_____

Now check your answers to determine your primary love language:

1. a. feelings	b. auditory	c. visual
2. a. feelings	b. auditory	c. visual
3. a. auditory	b. visual	c. feelings
4. a. visual	b. feelings	c. auditory
5. a. feelings	b. visual	c. auditory
6. a. visual	b. auditory	c. feelings
7. a. auditory	b. visual	c. feelings
8. a. auditory	b. feelings	c. visual
9. a. visual	b. auditory	c. feelings
10. a. visual	b. auditory	c. feelings
11. a. visual	b. auditory	c. feelings
12. a. auditory	b. visual	c. feelings
13. a. feelings	b. visual	c. auditory
14. a. feelings	b. auditory	c. visual
15. a. visual	b. feelings	c. auditory

Count the number of visual, auditory and feelings preferences for both you and your mate. The category which captured the most answers suggests your primary love language.

Me: Visual_____ Auditory_____ Feelings_____
Spouse: Visual_____ Auditory_____ Feelings_____ ²

We all see, hear and feel. But both you and your spouse have a dominant sense through which you prefer to receive communication. One of your primary missions as a husband or wife is to discover your spouse's dominant sense and center your communication in that area. Learn to speak the love language of your partner instead of insisting that he/she adapt to your love language. As you learn to communicate in your spouse's language, you will experience a great improvement in your relationship!

Speaking your spouse's language is not limited to vocabulary but also includes what I call an individual's packaging. Packaging refers to whether a person is an amplifier (sharing great volumes of details) or a condenser (sharing little more than the bottom line). If your partner is an amplifier, in addition to focusing on his seeing, hearing or feeling preference, give lots of information and detail. If he is a condenser, keep it brief. You can always expand if the condenser wants more.

Let's investigate each of these three senses more closely to find some ideas on how to communicate in specific love languages.

The Visual Person

The visual person (either male or female) relates to the world around him in terms of how things look to him. When he imagines he visualizes, and when he remembers, he recalls a picture. He experiences life through his eyes. He is primarily a watcher—movies, TV, sporting events, people, art exhibits or museums, scenery. He probably prefers reading, collecting items to look at, taking pictures, and looking at you. He is often concerned with how he looks to others. A visual person talks about how things look rather than how he feels. Often a visual person tends to withdraw and brood when upset rather than talking through the problem.

A visual person prefers face-to-face conversations over using the telephone and responds well to written messages. He wants to see a letter firsthand rather than have it read to him. A visual person who travels wants a map nearby and prefers to study it himself rather than have it read to him.

Convey your love to a visual person by giving him something he can see—a picture, an object, a love note, etc. He may be concerned with the way he looks to you and especially the way you look to him.

How can you tell if a person is visually oriented? Listen to the words he uses. Here is a list of statements that are more typical of a visual person:

> From my *point of view.*
> *I* see what you're driving at.
> That *looks* like a sure thing.
> That's really *clear* to me.
> What you're *picturing* is...
> I don't know; I've *drawn a blank.*
> *Show* me what you're getting at.
> There's a *clear pattern* to this.
> It's beginning to *dawn* on me.

What do all these words mean? If you are an astute salesperson, you will listen to the language of your customer and begin to respond in like manner. If you are an astute employer or employee, you will listen to your fellow workers and communicate in their language. If you are an astute minister, you will use more visuals in your sermons in order to bridge the gap to the visually oriented in the congregation. And if you are an astute spouse, you will begin to communicate your love in terms he/she can best appreciate and receive.

Here are some phrases you can use in response to the visual person:

> I'm beginning to *see* your point of view.
> That *looks* good to me.

What you shared with me really *lights up* my day.
You know, I can just *picture us* on the beach in Maui.

Practice using visually oriented words, especially if they are new to you. Write down a list of visual words—as many as possible—and look for ways to use them in conversation with your visually oriented spouse. If you usually say, "That *feels* good to me," change it to "That *looks* good to me" when you are talking with a visual person. You may feel awkward at first as you try out a new vocabulary. Continue to practice and you will soon feel at ease.

Don't expect your spouse to notice your change in vocabulary. He or she probably won't be consciously aware of a language improvement. But your visual spouse will feel more comfortable in relating to you, perhaps without even knowing why.

Men tend to be more visual than women; in fact, most men are visual persons. Women tend to lean toward feelings. But both men and women can learn to strengthen the two senses that are subordinate to the dominant language. Over the years the visual trait has been and still is my strong suit. But I have worked on the other two areas and now enjoy a greater balance.

If you live with a visual person you must adjust to his dominant style of perception. For example, if you are planning to buy new chairs for the family room, you will want to discuss with your spouse how the room's appearance will improve in addition to how comfortable the chairs will be. If you want to escape to a quiet retreat with no phones and few people, emphasize to your visual spouse the scenic aspects of the location. And for the sexual dimensions of marriage there are special applications of lovemaking to which the visual spouse is more inclined, but we will save that information until the next chapter.

The Auditory Person

The auditory person is interested in hearing about life. This individual relates more to sounds than sights. When he reads, the auditory person doesn't see pictures, he hears words. If your partner is auditory, don't expect him to notice a new article of clothing, hairdo, room arrangement or plant in the yard. You need to tell him more than you show him. He prefers talking about something to looking at it. Long conversations are important to the auditory spouse and they tend to remember what they hear better than others.

If you want to share feelings, the auditory person will best understand you if you verbalize them. Auditory people hear equally what is said and *not* said, and they are astute at picking up tonal changes and voice inflections. Harsh responses may be upsetting to them. The telephone is an important part of their lives.

Auditory people fall into two different categories. Some feel compelled to fill the silent moments of life with sound: talking, playing the stereo, humming, etc. But others prefer quiet. Why would an auditory person opt for silence? Because many of them are carrying on internal conversations and external sounds are an interruption. Sometimes a silent auditory person's spoken responses may not make sense to you because he fails to relate the full content of the conversation in his head.

Romancing an auditory partner must include saying "I love you" again and again. But since their hearing sense is so acute, *how* you say it is as important as *how often* you say it. Discover the words, phrases and tones that best convey your spoken love and use them often.

Romancing your hearing-oriented spouse also means suggesting activities that he would especially enjoy. Here is a suggested list of possible preferences:

Enjoying outdoor sounds
Talking, arguing, giving advice
Listening to the radio, music, concerts
Playing a musical instrument
Attending lectures, giving lectures, teaching
Operating CB or "ham" radio

Recording, writing or creating dialogs

Using the telephone

Let's consider some of the words and phrases an auditory person uses:

That *sounds* good to me.

Let's *talk* about this again.

Boy, that's *music* to my *ears!*

People seem to *tune* him out when he is talking.

Harmony is important to me.

I *hear* you *clear as a bell.*

Tell me a little more about it.

Give me a *call* so we can discuss the proposal.

Your *tone* of voice is coming through *loud and clear.*

What kind of responses should you use with an auditory person? The same type of words and phrases. Identify them, write them out and practice them. A simple change from "Doesn't that look *good* to you?" to "Doesn't that *sound* good to you?" will make a difference to an auditory person. Instead of asking, "Would you like to go *see* that new movie with me?" ask "How does attending that new movie *sound* to you?" Asking an auditory person to share his feelings may not provoke a response. But asking him to say what comes to mind when he hears the word "love," "romance," "sexy," or whatever will tap into his auditory style. Now you're speaking his language.

You may say, "Changing the way we talk to one another sounds like a pointless game that requires a lot of work." Work, yes; game, no. Effective communication requires being sensitive to, and diligently accommodating, the uniqueness of your partner. By learning new ways to talk we climb out of our communication ruts and become more flexible. Changing your style of communication can make the difference between holding your spouse's attention and being ignored. That would seem to be reason enough!

Does the auditory person have special needs and wants in the category of sex? Yes. But we will save that discussion until chapter 9. Please be patient!

The Feelings Person

Some people tend to be very feelings oriented, although it is more often true of women than men. Feelings people tend to touch a lot. They often desire to develop deep relationships. They crave closeness, love and affection. They are generally "right brain" people, operating more intuitively than logically or analytically. Physical comfort and bodily sensations are important parts of their language style.

Feelings people often show their feelings even though many of them do not verbalize their feelings well. You can usually read happiness, sadness, anger, love, or delight on their faces or hear these emotions in the tone of their voices. And they are concerned about how others feel toward them. A feelings oriented man who can effectively verbalize his emotions can be one of the easiest husbands to live with.

Feelings people are more spontaneous than auditory or visual people. This trait can be both positive and negative. On one hand they are free to create spur-of-the-moment, fun activities. But on the other hand they may, for no apparent logical reason, change their minds and upset the schedule of a plan-in-advance spouse.

Here are some words and phrases often used by a feelings oriented person. The word "feel," of course, will also be used in a variety of contexts:

I have some good *vibes* about this.
I have a *sense* about that.
I like to get *close* to you.
That person was so *sensitive.*
I'm so *happy* today. Yesterday I was *unhappy.*
I like being *near* you.

You will also hear words like *touch, tense, pressure, hurt, touchy, soft, smooth, handle,* and *relaxed* from a feelings person. Whereas the visual person says, "It *looks* good to me," and the auditory person says, "It *sounds* good to me," the feelings person will say, "It *feels* good to me," or "I'm *comfortable* with that," or "I understand how you *feel.*"

If you were a car salesman, and wanted to relate to a feelings oriented customer, you wouldn't say, "You really look good in that car." Nor would you pitch the car by saying, "Doesn't it sound quiet inside?" Rather you would say, "Don't you feel comfortable and relaxed behind the wheel? What a sensation it is to drive this car on the highway." You communicate with a feelings person through his emotions.

Romance your feelings-level spouse by suggesting activities that are filled with personal experience, social contact and emotional stimulation. Involve other sensations such as taste and smell. In fact, many feelings people, especially men, really enjoy food. A special meal in a restaurant or dining room with just the right ambiance can be very romantic.

Feelings people like to be known for their sensitivity. A wise spouse will notice this trait and comment on it often. Feelings people like to be touched often, especially when being spoken to. And, of course, chapter 9 will give added information on the sexual needs and wants of the feelings level spouse. (No fair skipping ahead or peeking!)

I switch forms of expression quite often when I am counseling. I may see eight different clients during the day, but I try to speak each person's specific language—visual, auditory or feelings. Remember the premarital counseling session with Bill and Jan I shared earlier in this chapter? Return to it now and answer the following questions based upon the three styles of language presented here. Pay special attention to the italicized words as you reread the conversation:

1. What is Bill's primary style of perception?

2. What is Jan's primary style of perception?

3. Why did I emphasize increasing my speech rate with Bill and speaking softly with Jan?

Mixed Marriages

What happens when two people with different perceptions marry? Let's consider some of the possible matchups and their results.

If a visual person marries an auditory person, the auditory person may not meet his partner's standards for dressing because he is less concerned with fashion. Also, the visual person may tend more toward neatness and orderliness in the household because of its visual attractiveness. The auditory person may forget the visible shopping list his spouse gives him, but will have better success remembering verbal lists and instructions.

What if the husband is visual and the wife is auditory? He attempts to *show* his love by buying her flowers and gifts and taking her places. Then one day she says, "You don't love me," and he is floored. He points to all the things he has given her, but she simply says, "You never tell me you love me." To the auditory wife, words are more important than gifts. Say the words, write the words or record them on a cassette tape for her to hear.

The auditory wife may also err by limiting her love of her visually oriented husband to words. He may appreciate his wife *telling* him of her love, but he will really get the message when his brain receives certain visual stimuli. Her attention to grooming and dress, neatness in the home, and pleasant sights rather than sounds will visually present her love.

Sometimes people come into my work area (or even my bathroom!) and rearrange my personal items. These people may think I won't notice, but I do. I have also made some people uncomfortable when, in a home or a doctor's office, I will take it upon myself to straighten a crooked picture on the wall. What does this say about me? Yes, I am more visually oriented.

Let's say a feelings man is married to a visual woman. He comes in the door and immediately grabs her, hugs her and cuddles her. She may pull away and say, "You're always grabbing me. All you want to do is touch. I'd like to go somewhere with you and, please, look at me instead of sneaking up behind me!"

Conversely, she needs to learn to talk to her husband through his feelings vocabulary. He needs touching, caressing and closeness to feel loved. He likes things to be comfortable and fit well more than being visually attractive. He wears an old shirt and a floppy hat that look awful to her but feel good to him. She must make room in her life for her husband's comfort need.

Some couples have clashed over buying new furniture. The visual spouse wants the room to look neat and new while the feelings person wants to feel good and comfortable in the room. The loving solution? Agreeing on furniture that is both neat and comfortable, meeting the needs of both partners.

The feelings person needs to respond to the visual spouse by talking about how he "sees" things. The visual partner, in turn, should learn to develop a "feel" for those things that are important to his partner. For example, here's a conversation between a feelings wife and a visual husband:

Marge: John, I really would like a new outfit for the conference we're attending. I just don't have anything that feels comfortable. Nothing feels right anymore.

John: But you seem to have several outfits in the closet that aren't very old and still look great. Why spend any more money?

Marge: But I just don't feel good in them. Do you know what I mean?

John: No, I don't. It appears to me you have lots of outfits that you don't wear that much. What's wrong with those?

Marge (who is beginning to see the light): John, you're right. I do have a number of outfits. But none of them look very good on me. And for this conference I want to look my best for you. Why don't I bring home two or three for you to see and we can go from there?

Guess what John said to that? There is a greater possibility that his response was affirmative because Marge was speaking his language.[3]

The Language Battle of the Sexes

Marge and John are not unusual. No matter what your dominant sense, most husbands and wives have difficulty communicating. But if a husband and wife are ever to achieve any degree of intimacy, and feel loved and understood by his or her partner, they will have to learn to break the barrier of male/female communication differences.

In all cultures throughout the world, there are linguistic differences between men and women, both in style and substance. In our own culture men tend to resist expressing themselves directly. Many wives are frustrated because their husbands only hint about certain things, rather than speaking about them directly. This is especially true when it comes to areas involving expression of feelings; answering personal questions like, "What's bothering you?"; or vocalizing their love.

The topic of feelings is a major source of frustration in couple relationships. Most men do not have a feeling vocabulary, and thus putting into words what they are experiencing is a real chore. The husband often hides his feelings behind a facade of facts, which only serves to further distance him from his wife's feelings. Men tend to talk more about tasks and facts than feelings, reflecting their tendency to be goal-oriented.

This primarily male trait also carries over into communication. A husband's response to what his wife may consider an intimate conversation is, "What's the purpose here?" or "What will this accomplish?" Men want an agenda. They tend to give a one-two-three solution to problems—even when no one requested an answer! Whereas a woman tends to empathize, men want to be in control, in conversation as well as other areas of life.

Men tend to interrupt more than women. And if a man initiates a conversation with his wife, there is a 96 percent chance that the conversation will continue; if his wife initiates the conversation, there is only a 36 percent chance it will continue.

In the choice of words, women tend to use more descriptive words, more adverbs of intensity. The descriptive adjectives used by men and women vary significantly. You seldom hear men talking about the "beautiful mauve drapes" or the "gorgeous sunset, streaked with lavender." Women use terms like taupe, beige, violet and mauve to describe an item, whereas a man may describe the same item as "red" or "green."

A man might describe an event or experience as "fine," while his wife might describe it in several sentences, with her choice of words and inflections painting a very descriptive picture. This frustrates so many wives, who feel they can't get close to their husbands because they are on different wavelengths. The scarcity of words, minimal inflections, and little or no emotion used by men lend themselves to a sterile conversation.[4]

It is impossible to separate intimacy from communication. Notice the five levels of communication and the level of intimacy in the diagram below.

With many couples one person may communicate at level five, the other at level two. They just can't connect, and therefore end up frus-

Level 1	Level 2	Level 3	Level 4	Level 5
Lowest Intimacy	Low Intimacy	Moderate Intimacy	High Intimacy	Highest Intimacy
Facts, Information	Idea of Others	Your Own Ideas and Opinions	Personal Information About Yourself	Your Feelings and Emotions

trated. It is imperative that both learn to communicate at level five for true intimacy to develop.

Often I have described people as amplifiers or condensers. The amplifiers give a number of descriptive sentences as they talk, while condensers give one or two sentences. In approximately 70 percent of marriages, the man is the condenser and the woman is the amplifier. Neither is a bad trait, but the amplifier wishes his/her partner would share more, while the condenser wishes his/her partner would share less. It is only when each adapts the style of their partner when talking together that real communication occurs.

Women simply enjoy hearing more details than men. One woman voiced her frustration in this manner: "How come there's no give and take in a conversation with a man? Sometimes it's like trying to play tennis with no one in the other court?"[5]

The question often arises, "Who talks more, men or women?" The stereotype depicts women as talking more, which they do in private or personal conversations. For a woman, the language of conversation is basically a language of rapport. Men, on the other hand, talk more in public speaking, meetings, etc., and their conversation is more "report talk," focusing on accomplishing a task.[6]

When men and women talk to one another, both make adjustments, but women make more than men. They are also influenced by the men's topics and tend to follow their lead.[7]

Women tend to ask more questions than men. This seems to indicate they are willing to take more responsibility in facilitating and sustaining conversations. Men are less likely to ask questions, especially of a personal nature. Questions are basically a request for information. Many men tend to make the assumption, "If she has anything to say to me, she'll say it without my having to ask." But many women feel, "If I don't ask him, he'll think I don't care. And I may not discover something important."[8]

Timing, pacing, pausing and agenda difference in listening may complicate a couple's attempts to develop ongoing intimacy. If the husband uses intermittent pauses when talking or speaks at a slower pace, his partner (if she is the opposite) may jump in with her own thoughts or tend to hurry her husband along. Understanding and accepting these differences can be very beneficial to the relationship.

Unfortunately, some individuals are simply overly long talkers and can never seem to get to the point. They fail to identify the subject, ramble around the barn several times, and give unnecessary details. If his/her spouse is a linear communicator who identifies the subject immediately, he/she will be especially put off by this style. And often this person falsely believes he or she is communicating effectively.

Even listening reflects a difference in style between men and women. Men tend to offer verbal responses quite infrequently, and when they do they are meant to indicate, "I agree with you." But women interpret these statements to mean, "I am listening." Why? Because women give much more frequent response when someone is talking to them, and this means or signifies they are listening to the person talking. Thus a wife may feel as if her husband isn't listening to her, when in reality he is simply more of a passive listener.[9]

In summary, every couple must find a mutual language or communication style if they are ever going to establish any level of intimacy in their relationship. But once they make the commitment to achieve that mutual communication style, the results are so exciting that it is worth all the effort.

Notes

1. H. Norman Wright, *Energize Your Life Through Total Communication* (Old Tappan, NJ: Fleming H. Revell, 1986), pp. 50-53.
2. Tracy Cabot, *How to Keep a Man in Love with You Forever* (New York: McGraw-Hill Co., 1986), pp. 111-113. Used by permission.
3. Material in this chapter adapted from: Jerry Richardson and Joel Margulis, *The Magic of Rapport* (San Francisco: Harbor Publications, out of print); Robert Dilts, *Applications of Neuro-Linguistic Programming* (Cupertino, CA: Meta Publications, 1983); Tracy Cabot, *How to Keep a Man in Love with You Forever* (New York: McGraw-Hill Co., 1986).
4. Steven Naifeh and Gregory White Smith, *Why Can't Men Open Up?* (New York: Warner Books, 1985), pp. 70-115, adapted.
5. Rubin, Lillian B., *Just Friends* (New York: Harper & Row, 1985), p. 105.

6. Deborah Tannen, *You Just Don't Understand* (New York: William Morrow and Co., 1990), pp. 76-77, adapted.
7. Ibid., pp. 236-237, adapted.
8. Aaron T. Beck, *Love Is Never Enough* (New York: Harper and Row, 1988), p. 80, adapted.
9. Ibid., pp. 74-75, adapted.

NINE

Rejoice in Your Sexuality!

L ord, it's hard to know what sex really is—
Is it some demon put here to torment me?
Or some delicious seducer from reality?
It is neither of these, Lord.
I know what sex is—
It is body and spirit,
It is passion and tenderness,
It is strong embrace and gentle hand-holding,
It is open nakedness and hidden mystery,
It is joyful tears in honeymoon faces, and
It is tears on wrinkled faces at a golden
wedding anniversary.
Sex is a quiet look across the room,
a love note on a pillow,
a rose laid on a breakfast plate,
laughter in the night.
Sex is life—not all of life—
but wrapped up in the meaning of life.
Sex is your good gift, O God
To enrich life,
To continue the race,

To communicate,
To show me who I am,
To reveal my mate,
To cleanse through "one flesh."
Lord, some people say sex and religion don't mix;
But your Word says sex is good.
Help me to keep it good in my life.
Help me to be open about sex
    And still protect its mystery.
Help me to see that sex
Is neither demon nor deity.
Help me not to climb into a fantasy world
    Of imaginary sexual partners;
Keep me in the real world
    To love the people you have created.

Teach me that my soul does not have to frown
    at sex
    for me to be a Christian.
It's hard for many people to say, "Thank God for sex!"
Because for them sex is more a problem than a gift.
    They need to know that sex and gospel
Can be linked together again.
They need to hear the good news about sex.
Show me how I can help them.

Thank you, Lord, for making me a sexual being.
Thank you for showing me how to treat others
with trust and love.
Thank you for letting me talk to you about sex.
Thank you that I feel free to say:
    "Thank God for sex!"[1]

Sex—God's Invention

Where did sex come from? Since God created all things (see John 1:1-3), we know that He created sex. It was His idea, not man's. Like everything else that God made, sex is to be celebrated, enjoyed and used properly.

What is sex for? Human sexual activity has several purposes. Sex is the vehicle God designed for the continuation of the race. Procreation is a very important function of sex and, unfortunately, even today some people believe it's the only function of sex. But having babies is not the only reason we have sex.

Sex is also for recreation. That may come as a shock to some but God also designed sex for the pleasure of a husband and wife. The Scriptures encourage the enjoyment and sensual delights of sex within the boundaries of a marriage relationship. The Song of Solomon is the prime example, celebrating the physical love between a man and a woman in passion-filled poetry. It is interesting to note that the Scriptures often use poetic language to describe sexual organs, drives, energies, desires and outlets. For example, a favorite symbol for sex in the Bible is water fountains, streams, cisterns, springs and wells. Have you ever shared with your spouse what you enjoy most about your sexual relationship? Has your mate ever shared his/her thoughts on the subject with you? This discussion topic, coupled with a Bible study on some of the terms above, might create an interesting evening's experience for you!

Contrary to what some Christians think, God is not against pleasure. He created your body, including its sexual parts, and equipped you with a nervous system which enables you to experience pleasure. However, it must be kept in mind that pleasure is a by-product in life and not the ultimate goal. In the process of serving God wholeheartedly with productive lives and ministries, we are free to enjoy the pleasures of sex with the partner He gives us.

Sexual pleasure was designed by God to be enjoyed within the sanctity of the marriage relationship. Indeed, the expression of sex in marriage is a form of communication. Sex is a means for expressing the deep unity that a husband and wife feel toward one another. Sex is a powerful force that includes ecstatic physical release. Even the pleasurable sensations of orgasm and ejaculation were God's ideas!

Problems with Sex

But not everyone has an easy time with sex. Read the following paragraphs thoughtfully:

> The average Christian has an especially hard time integrating his sexuality with his faith. He is dedicated to a Lord whose earthly life was celibate and whose messengers were not interested in reporting his attitudes toward sex. He is summoned to follow the Lord into purity and holiness, neither of which is usually allowed to include an enthusiastic summons to sexual fulfillment. He is informed and guided by Scripture, whose word on sexuality is not always specific and clear. He senses that he ought not to feel right about anything that his Lord feels less than enthusiastic about. Does God like sex? Would Jesus be pleased with our restless urge, our fantasies, our irrational itching for sexual experience? Can we integrate sexuality with Christian sanctification? Can a Christian person think about the mystery of his own sexuality and rejoice and be glad in it?
>
> Some Christians feel that their sexuality is nature's strongest competitor for their loyalty to Christ: "You cannot love both God and sex." While they may not make it part of their creed, their feelings tell them that sexuality is not a sweet gift of creation but a bitter fruit of the fall. They are supported in this by a long antisexual tradition within Christianity.
>
> Augustine, to whom we otherwise owe more than most of us even imagine, interpreted the Christian's calling to struggle against evil as a calling to struggle against their sexuality. Intense desire for sexual fulfillment and intense pleasure from

sexual action were for him marks of fallen man. Augustine could not imagine an innocent person in Paradise turned on sexually: a sinless Adam could never have been sexually aroused by a pure Eve; Adam and Eve could not have walked with God in the day and made spontaneous love at night. If we do this now it is only because we have not brought our bodies under the rule of Christ. The less one is driven toward sex and the less pleasure he receives from sexual expression, the more sure he can be of his own sanctification. The Lord, in his grace, tolerates our inconsistency; but we must know that he calls us to better, sexless things. This was how Augustine felt about sexuality. Some Christians still carry Augustine's feelings in their hearts; they can only hope that God tolerates their sexuality until their liberation from it in heaven.[2]

Some people believe that all sex should be repressed because it is evil. Where did this nonsense come from? It came from the belief that the body was an evil house that had taken over the soul. Thus the needs of the body must be denied so the spirit can be dominant.

There are not too many people left in our country who think this way, but the Shakers of past history certainly did. The Shakers were celibates who believed that the body was a source of evil. Marriage was allowed but sexual relations within marriage were considered sinful. During the Civil War the Shakers adopted orphans as a means to continue their existence as a sexless sect.

A few years ago I had the opportunity to visit the historical headquarters of the Shakers. I noticed that their houses even had separate staircases to the second floor—one for husbands and one for wives.

In spite of Scripture's clarity on the subject, a destructive negativism regarding sex has found its way into the thinking and teaching of the Church over the years. The following statements summarize some of this errant thinking:

Sexual sins are the worst kind of sins in the eyes of God.

Pleasure, even from allowable sexual acts, is unwholesome for
the believer.
Sexual desire itself is a result of sin.
Celibacy is holier than marriage.
The first sin was somehow sexual in nature.
Marriage is just a remedy for sin.
The body and all material things are displeasing to God.
Refraining from intercourse in marriage is pleasing to God.

The attitude of sexual negativism has continued in the Church
through the centuries but was actually much stronger in the early life of
the Church. Early Church fathers seem to have overlooked the positive,
biblical teachings about sex. Jerome, for example, would not permit
married couples to partake of the Lord's Supper for several days after
performing what he called the "bestial act" of intercourse. "A wise man
ought to love his wife with judgment, not with passion," he wrote,
adding, "He who too ardently loves his own wife is an adulterer."
Ambrose made a similar statement and was quoted with approval by
Augustine and much later by John Calvin in his commentary on the
seventh commandment.

Jerome told husbands, "If we abstain from coitus we honor our
wives; if we do not abstain, well, what is the opposite of 'honor' but
'insult'?" Gradually there even emerged among some early Christians
a strange new form of marriage—"spiritual" or "continent" marriage,
in which husbands and wives made solemn pacts of virginity. They
promised to "keep their bodies for Christ" by not having sexual relations. Couples continued to live together, but in some sort of broth-
er-sister arrangement. I don't think this approach would work so well
today!

By the Middle Ages the Church's teaching on sex had reached thoroughly unbiblical extremes. Peter Lombard and Gratien warned Christians that the Holy Spirit left the room when a married couple engaged
in sexual intercourse—even if for the purposes of conceiving a child.
Other Church leaders insisted that God required sexual abstinence dur-

ing all holy days and seasons. Furthermore, couples were advised to shun sex on Thursdays in honor of Christ's arrest, Fridays in memory of His crucifixion, Saturdays in honor of the Virgin Mary, Sundays in remembrance of Christ's resurrection, and Mondays out of respect for departed souls. Sex was only allowed on Tuesdays and Wednesdays. Guess which days of the week were the favorites!

The Church sought to regulate every facet of life, leaving no room for the individual's right to determine God's will, nor the rights of the married couple to create their own life-style.[3]

Christians need to adopt the biblical perspective of sex, and the Bible teaches that sex is good. The New Testament approves of sex and marriage. Jesus attended the wedding in Cana and performed His first miracle there in order to make the occasion more joyful (see John 2:1-11). His presence there can be taken as a stamp of approval on the institution of marriage and the joy that accompanies it.

Jesus compared His presence on earth to that of a bridegroom at a marriage feast. He criticized those who suggested that gloom or sadness should mark such an occasion (see Mark 2:18-20). John the Baptist used the same picture in referring to Jesus (see John 3:29).

Furthermore, we cannot overlook the words of Jesus Himself, which beautifully describe the order of creation in which men and women marry, establish homes and families (see Matt. 19:4-6). Sexual expression in marriage is also taught in Ephesians 5:22-33; Hebrews 13:4; 1 Corinthians 7:3-5; and 1 Thessalonians 4:1-8.

The Sexual Christian

When God created us He equipped us with the capacity for both pain and pleasure. Children discover pain through countless bumps, falls and scrapes. And many children experience their first sexual pleasure as they explore their own bodies. Such exploration and discovery is very normal.

The pleasure of sex in the Old Testament is closely associated with the joy of bearing children. God told Eve that her desire (elsewhere translated "craving") for her husband would be so strong that she would be willing to obey him and to suffer the pains of childbirth for the sake of this yearning and attraction (see Gen. 3:16). Sarah reacted to the promise of a son in her old age by saying, "After I am worn out . . . will I now have this pleasure?" (Gen. 18:12, *NIV*), which may be referring to the gratification of her sexual desire.

Isaac and Rebekah also shared the pleasure of sex. It was the scene of Isaac caressing ("sporting" in the *King James Version;* making love to

---

God not only created the pleasurable drives within us but also the proper context for their complete expression and fulfillment.

---

her) Rebekah that indicated to Abimelech that they were husband and wife instead of brother and sister as Isaac said (see Gen. 26:8,9). Approval of sexual pleasure is also implied in the regulation that a newly married man was exempt from military service for one year (see Deut. 24:5), in the proverbial advice to rejoice in a youthful wife (see Prov. 5:18) and in the obviously dominant theme of the sheer delight of sex in the Song of Solomon (see 1:2; 2:6,7; 4:5; 7:1-3 for example).

Husbands and wives in biblical times were free to enjoy sexual satisfaction as they saw fit. Both frequency and style of expression were open to personal choice. As suggested in Genesis 26:8, caressing, or sexual foreplay, was quite acceptable. In Song of Solomon 7:1-3, the poet spoke of gazing with rapture upon his lover's breasts and navel. In Proverbs 5:18,19, the young man is encouraged to rejoice in his wife, to be satisfied in her breasts always and captivated by her love.

Do you thank God for sex? I don't only mean sex in general, but also the specific details of your sexual enjoyment with your mate. Do you thank God together for each other's body and the pleasure God allows you to experience with each other? Can you pray the following prayer? Can you pray it aloud in the presence of your spouse?

Thank you, O Creator, for the gift of sex to enrich human life.

I rejoice in the wonder of a man and a maid,
    in the laughter of lovers,
    in the fragility of puppy love,
    in the excitement of "one-flesh."
Teach me to celebrate the beauty of bodies,
    the warmth of holding hands,
    the sweetness of Valentine's kisses,
    the joyfulness of sex.
Spare me from the anti-bodies
    who are ashamed of themselves and your creation.
Waken me to the goodness of my body,
    And help me to cherish my body as your gift.
Melt the stiffness of my soul, and
    Do not let me be ashamed of passion.
Help me to see that I can be
    sensual and pure,
    happy and holy,
    sexual and spiritual.
I affirm your creation, O God,
    the seeds spring forth,
    trees growing leaves,
    flowers blooming,
    bodies filling out,
    babies being born.
Remind me, O Creator, that sex comes from you
    And not from the devil,
    No matter what the prudes may say.
Make me lighthearted, O God,

Let me be sensual but not sinful;
Let me dance and sing and be silly.
Keep my desires rich and real.
Do not let my nerves go dead
And my feelings get jaded.
Help me to celebrate sex as a good part of your
    creation.
Teach me to say: "Thank God for sex."[4]

When Jesus Christ enters a person's life, He enables that individual to start living with a new spiritual dimension. The more a Christian grows in his faith, the more his attitudes and behaviors become fulfilling to him and to God.

But what about sex? Are there any sexual benefits to being a Christian? Many people view Christianity as being sexually restrictive rather than freeing, sexually negative rather than positive. Some see God as anti-sex rather than pro-sex. But I submit to you that God is pro-sex. It was *His* idea. God not only created the pleasurable drives within us but also the proper context for their complete expression and fulfillment.

For many Christians, faith and sexuality exist like the two rails of a train track. They parallel each other as far as the eye can see but they never come together. Are there any sexual advantages or benefits to being a Christian? The answer is yes!

First, negative attitudes toward our bodies and sex can be overcome by accepting what God has said about them. When we realize that God is aware of our lovemaking as a married couple and is saying, "That is the way I intended it!" we can rest in God's approval. God wants you to experience sexual pleasure as a married couple. Ecstasy and joy are His gift to you! The fullness of pleasure, without guilt from exploitation or the violation of another person's integrity, leaves a couple with a deep sense of contentment and satisfaction. Your pleasure is both physical and relational. The pleasing afterglow of a sexual encounter includes the contented awareness that the lovemaking enjoyed was blessed and approved by God.

Second, the presence of Christ in our lives can give us the ability to love each other with *agape* love. Because of God's unconditional love within us, we can exercise accepting, unconditional love, which brings greater sexual pleasure in our marriages. *Agape* love moves us from "What can I *get* out of this encounter?" to "What can I *give* in order to please my partner in this encounter?" Christians should be able to learn

---

It is easy to let a vital part of our marriages become routine! The busy pace and multiple distractions of our lives tend to interfere with our sexual expression.

---

the rewarding balance of sexually pleasing their mates while being sexually pleased by their mates.

Third, the potential for greater commitment to one another is available because of the presence of Christ in our lives. As we learn to trust Him and accept the true worth He places on our lives, we can relinquish the insecurities and fears that often keep married partners from total commitment to each other. In turn, commitment freely given and received heightens the sexual experience.

Fourth, as we experience Jesus' acceptance of us, He helps us to communicate with our partners in an open and honest manner. A knowledge of God's acceptance leads to greater personal security and self-acceptance, diminishing fear of rejection. Vulnerability can occur and hidden hurts and concerns can come to the forefront to be dealt with. The elimination of these barriers creates a closer relationship and a richer sexual life.

Fifth, God's forgiveness leads to a greater sexual fulfillment in marriage. Having been forgiven by God, we learn to forgive ourselves and others. A marriage relationship in which forgiveness is mutually sought and offered will be blessed with a satisfying intimacy that will energize the sexual dimension.

Romans 8:1 states, "There is now no condemnation for those who are in Christ Jesus" *(NIV)*. Many Christians have no trouble with condemnation *except* in sexual matters. I have counseled numerous individuals who say, "I know the Scripture states that I'm forgiven. I know it and feel it—except when it comes to sex. For some reason, I still feel guilty over what I did in high school. On Sundays I heard, 'You better not do it,' and I would nod my head in agreement. But on Friday night I would do it. I wished I hadn't. It seems like sex sins are the worst."

But the good news is that even our past sexual sins can be forgiven. I have asked some individuals to write a letter of confession to Jesus requesting forgiveness. Then I suggest that they sit in a chair and imagine that Jesus is coming into the room. I ask them to hold the letter out in their hands and imagine Jesus receiving it and saying, "You are forgiven. Accept and experience my forgiveness. You don't need to blame yourself any more." In time the burden of guilt is lifted.

Dwight Small summarizes the preceding benefits a Christian enjoys in the sexual dimension in this way: "So, properly experienced within marriage and its commitment to fidelity, the sexual relation brings a sense of well-being, complete identity, joy unbounded, perfect mutuality, freedom in responsibility, fulfillment of purpose, and an indescribable unity of being."[5]

Let's Get Touchy

Sexual touching is a vital part of a husband-wife relationship. But as with other forms of marital communication, touching takes time and effort to develop. The intense drive for physical contact that precedes the wedding, and lasts for a while afterwards, often turns into a rut: "Well, it's Thursday night. I guess it's time to have sex again."

Each of you will differ in your desire for the expression of physical love. One of you may enjoy a great amount of bodily contact while the other is satisfied with much less. Your specific tastes for touching may also be different. One may enjoy passionate embraces, caresses and massages while the other prefers more relaxed contact such as resting his head on his partner's lap. One may like holding hands for an hour, the other for two minutes.

In order to increase the enjoyment of physical touching in your marriage, evaluate your present experience with touching. After each of you have completed the following statements, share your response with each other:

Some of the ways I like to be touched are...

Some of the ways I do not like to be touched are...

I think you like to be touched by...

The times I like to be touched are...

The times I prefer not to be touched are...

I think we touch each other ____ times each day.

Who does the most touching in our relationship?

Who prefers to do the touching in our relationship?

When I am touched it makes me feel...

When you are touched you feel...

The way we could improve our touching would be to...[6]

In addition to adjusting to each other's patterns of touching, couples need to learn the critical art of timing in their physical relationship. The following conversation is representative of scores I have heard in my office on the issue of timing:

"Norm, I think there's something else we need to address that is a little hard for Nancy to talk about," Fred continued.

"What do you mean 'hard for Nancy'?" Fred's wife bristled. "I think you avoid it just as much."

There was a long pause and I looked from one to the other and waited. Finally Nancy spoke up: "It's sex. It just isn't working, and after five years of marriage I'd like to know why not."

"That's what I want to know—why not?" Fred added. "Before we were married we had to wear handcuffs to keep us from getting into trouble. Then during the first year it was super. But now, what's going on?"

"Part of it is work," Nancy said. "We come home so exhausted half the time and our timing is lousy. I like sex at night, but you're too tired. Then you want to make love in the morning, and I'm too tired. I like to be awake to enjoy it!"

"It sounds as though timing is a major problem," I responded. "What about before dinner as an appetizer or after dinner as a dessert?"

They both laughed. "I'm serious," I continued. "You don't have any children yet. Perhaps it would work out. Have you ever considered these possibilities?" They both said no, but agreed that they were willing to experiment.

Nancy introduced another concern. "Another big problem is routineness. There's no romance like before. I don't want Fred to come up to me, grab my arm and say, 'Let's make love!' I want the atmosphere, the conversation, the time together to set the mood, and then I can really respond. I think we need to look at the calendar, set aside time for courting and come alive sexually again. But I don't want to be the only one doing the romancing."

"You're right," Fred replied. "I hate to schedule our lovemaking, but one romantic evening a week would be a lot better than our twice a week mechanical routine."

How easy it is to let a vital part of our marriages become routine! The busy pace and multiple distractions of our lives tend to interfere with our sexual expression. Is a clean house really more important that a romantic sexual encounter? Is one more appointment at the office a valid trade-off for time together in bed? Is the last hour of TV a valued substitute for physical enjoyment? Are you unconsciously collaborating to avoid sex?

Time demands do occur with growing families and businesses. And different body chemistries, which create the "night person" and the "morning person," can work against your sexual fulfillment. But these obstacles can be overcome. Make your sexual experience a mutual priority and leap the hurdles together. Each couple will need to determine their unique timing and style. Preplanned "love appointments" need not take the fun, excitement and spontaneity out of making love. Rather scheduling creates anticipation and allows time for conversation, foreplay, full arousal, release and affirmation afterward. Mutual planning and creativity can revitalize a sleepy sex life.

Sex Through the Ages

Let's consider another important topic that relates to sexual fulfillment between husband and wife. There is an interesting difference in the aging process of a man and a woman and a predictable effect that age has upon sex. Men reach their sexual peak in their late teens. For example, an 18-year-old man can have multiple orgasms quite easily with little recovery time needed in between. But a man at 50 may need to wait 12 to 24 hours before he is able to have another orgasm.

Women start sexually slower than men. Their sexual desire is usually lower in the teens and early 20s, not reaching full capacity until their 30s or early 40s. However, a woman's capacity for multiple orgasms does not change with age. A woman can have multiple orgasms throughout her adult life.

Couples in their 20s must realize that there is a biological reason why the wife may not want sex as often as the husband. It has nothing to do with her love for him, unless he is using sex as a weapon or a means of control.

Men in their 20s are strongly sexually oriented. They think, talk and fantasize about sex. This has a lot to do with their identity as males. Men want to communicate to others, "I am a man." Sexual thoughts flit in and out of a young man's mind all day long. Men think and dream about sex more than most women realize.

Women in their 20s place a high priority on intimacy in their relationship with a man. Intimacy involves a closeness and understanding, which may be communicated with a look or the touch of the hand. It is an invisible bond between a man and woman that is both physical and psychological. For her, intimacy is based in that special sense of belonging.

But for him, intimacy simply means one thing—sex! In a man's mind, taking the time to create a romantic atmosphere through ample conversation is a necessary evil he must endure on the way to sex. His intense sexual interest at this stage does not mean that he sees his wife as nothing more than a sex object; he simply has a high sexual drive.

Men do not crave a woman's type of intimate closeness in their 20s. Why? Perhaps because so much of their time is given to becoming

---

Sex is intended to be an expression of love, but unfortunately many men and women use sex to punish, reject, frustrate or disappoint their partners.

---

somebody and establishing a career identity. It is unfortunate that so many young men sacrifice the intimacy of their marriage relationship on the altar of self and career development.

During the 30s a man's and woman's sex drive tends to equal out. But in the 40s and 50s an interesting reversal occurs. Often during these years a wife is more interested in sex than her husband and she may feel rejected if he does not show the same interest.

Many women in their 40s attribute an increased sexual vigor to menopause, fewer family demands, enjoyment of work, and freedom from the restrictions of children in the home. What do women want from their men during their 40s? Once again it is intimacy. A man can be fat or skinny, with straight hair or no hair—physical appearance isn't that important. But he must be romantic and capable of intimacy. And intimacy for the 40-plus woman has changed slightly. Now she wants to know that she is important and desirable to her man. And she wants these messages to be clear-cut and direct.

Sex in the 50s takes on a different complexion. The young married man describes the ideal woman in terms of beauty, curves in the right places and sexiness. But the middle-aged husband places more importance on his woman's values and personality. Characteristics such as sensitivity, understanding, warmth, kindness and generosity fill the top of the list. Husbands in the 50s still want their wives to look good, but they are no longer hung up on her being a perfect "10."

Good Married Sex

Lovemaking in marriage involves three phases of physical response: desire, excitement and orgasm. Each is a separate entity. Sexual desire comes from a special neural system in the brain. Excitement results from the reflex vasodilation of genital blood vessels. Orgasm is dependent upon the reflex contractions of some specific genital muscles. But all three functions blend together to produce fulfilling sex.

If for some reason one of these responses is inhibited or "switched off," problems occur. Dr. Helen Kaplan, a well-known sex therapist, says, "One set of causes is likely to 'blow the fuse' of the orgasm circuits, while another type of conflict may 'disconnect the erection wires', while a different group of variables is likely to cause interference in the 'libido circuits' of the brain."[7]

Two main inhibitors of the desire phase are fear and hostility. The presence of these inhibitors can create physical response problems. Sex is intended to be an expression of love, but unfortunately many men and women use sex to punish, reject, frustrate or disappoint their partners. Often negative feelings such as anger and resentment in a marriage show up in the bedroom. If these attitudes are not properly dealt with they can lead to serious blockades to desire, excitement and orgasm.

There are three vital steps to achieving good married sex. Every couple needs to take these steps if they hope to realize sexual satisfaction.

First, every couple needs complete, accurate and thorough medical information on the subject of sex. No matter how much you feel you

may know or how varied your sexual experiences have been, I feel it
is essential for married couples of any age to listen to the tape series by
Dr. Ed Wheat, *Sex Techniques and Sex Problems in Marriage.* In addition, one of the finest books available on the Christian perspective of
sex is *The Gift of Sex* (Word), by Joyce and Cliff Penner.

Second, every couple needs to develop a healthy biblical perspective on sex. One of the assignments I have for you in this regard is to
read "The Most Beautiful Love Song Ever Written" to each other aloud
one evening. You will find this love song at the end of chapter 10.

Third, every husband and wife needs to learn to romance and love
his/her mate physically in the ways that person enjoys. Let's consider
this last necessity in detail.

Sadly, most men do not fully understand what women enjoy in
lovemaking, nor do they understand a woman's perspective on sex. A
few years ago Dr. Kevin Leman wrote a book titled, *Sex Begins in the
Kitchen* (Regal). Some people reacted negatively to that title, but it is so
accurate! The act of sexual intercourse is at the end of a continuum in
which non-erotic touches, hand holding, verbal affirmations and comments, winks, and assistance around the house during the day become
the foreplay. Yes, these acts and words of kindness and caring are part
of the sexual experience since the message conveyed to the woman is,
"I care for you and love you all day long, not just in the bedroom." A
woman also wants to know that her husband *likes* her. That's foreplay
too. But what about afterplay?

Sex researchers James Halperna and Mark Sherman surveyed thousands of women for their book, *Afterplay.* Their research indicated that
the single most important key to a woman's satisfaction was her partner's attitude *after* lovemaking.

A man's sexual response peaks during orgasm and then drops off
sharply. But a woman's response diminishes gradually. If after orgasm
a man leaves right away, turns on the TV or rolls over and falls asleep,
a woman feels cut off. But if he is content to lie close to her, caress her
and talk with her, she feels loved. The research showed that only 19
percent of the women identified orgasm as the most satisfying element

in sex. Most women preferred the closeness and caring of afterplay. These moments of tenderness assure a woman that she is not just a sexual object to be abandoned once the man has fulfilled his need.[8]

Dr. Ed Wheat has identified a number of additional male tendencies that hinder a wife's enjoyment of sex and should be avoided:

> The husband's stimulation of his wife during foreplay is mechanical rather than spontaneous.
>
> The husband is more interested in perfecting physical technique than in achieving emotional intimacy.
>
> The husband seems overly anxious for his wife to have an orgasm because that reflects upon his success as a lover, instead of simply wanting to please her and give her enjoyment whether it results in an orgasm or not.
>
> The husband fails to provide manual stimulation for his wife to have another orgasm after intercourse, even though she desires it.
>
> The husband is repetitious and boring in his approach.
>
> The husband is not sensitive to his wife's preferences.
>
> The husband seems too deadly serious about sex.[9]

Another real turn-off for both men and women is a partner who is physically out of shape. In light of the fact that our bodies are the temples of the Holy Spirit, the way we treat our bodies is vitally important. Christians can condemn the abuses of alcohol and tobacco all they want to, but overeating and lack of exercise are just as much of a problem for both longevity of life and sexual gratification. I'm not saying that exercising to condition the body and build muscle tone is always enjoyable. But a positive attitude and a firm commitment to a program of exercise will reap a payoff in your sex life.

Seven years ago I finally embarked on a fitness program that has become a mainstay of my life today. I don't always like working out on my Exercycle, but after pedaling close to 19,000 miles on it my energy level and muscle tone are greatly increased. And those nine miles each morning are not boring since I have a pile of reading material available as well as the stereo to listen to.

Many individuals who have "shaped up" say that their increased energy level and positive feelings about themselves contributed to increased sexual activity with their mates. And some spouses who exercise together, then come home to shower and relax, find their frequency of sexual expression and satisfaction level have dramatically increased. Try it—you might like it!

Now let's discuss briefly the relationship between sex and your language style. The visual person takes his tendency into the bedroom as well as every other room. The visual person (and remember that most men tend to be highly visual) is aroused by what he sees and he appreciates visual detail. The decor of the bedroom as well as what a spouse wears (or doesn't wear) is part of the process of creating romance. All visual people are not responsive to the same sights. It is important for the visual spouse to share with his mate the kinds of visual stimuli he appreciates. And if you have a visual spouse, ask him what sights are pleasing to him, and allow time for him to look at you.

Attention to visual details is important at all stages of a romantic evening that leads to sexual expression. A restaurant that captures a romantic atmosphere with lighting, warm colors, comfortable furniture, and so on is part of the foreplay that leads to a fulfilling sexual encounter.

An auditory person may take for granted all your efforts to look good, but he will enjoy romantic music on the stereo. This is usually the time for soft, soothing music rather than a Sousa march! And don't forget to disengage the telephone when it's time for lovemaking. The auditory partner is especially distracted by annoying sounds and interruptions.

Also, verbal expressions may be more important to this person, even during lovemaking. But be sure your auditory partner *wants* your verbal expressions at this time. The bottom line of romance is always doing those things that your spouse wants and avoiding those things your spouse dislikes.

A feelings man or woman will respond best to the feel of various fabrics, the touch of the skin and fragrances such as after shave lotion, perfume and massage oils. Whereas a visual person may respond to the subdued atmosphere of dim candlelight, the feelings person likes the fragrance of the candle. Room temperature is also very important to the feelings individual.

We all enjoy most forms of stimulation to some degree, but each of us finds some things more romantic than others. What do you prefer? Have you really identified your specific sexual needs in this way and shared them with your spouse? Have you asked him or her about specific preferences? If not, why not do it soon? You may be pleased and delighted with the information you receive!

Your sexual relationship will be enhanced by openly sharing your feelings and by thanking God for His wonderful gift. Read this concluding prayer, then consider reading it aloud with your spouse the next time you come together sexually. A new dimension will be added to your intimate expression.

> Thank you, O Redeemer,
> for letting me express love through sex.
> Thank you for making it possible
> for things to be right with sex—
> that there can be beauty and wonder
> between woman and man.
> You have given us a model for love in Jesus.
> He lived and laughed and accepted his humanity.
> He resisted sexual temptations
> Which were every bit as real as mine.
> He taught about the relationship of husband and wife
> By showing love for his bride the church.
> Thank you that he gives me
> the power to resist temptations also.
> Thank you that real sexual freedom
> comes in being bound to the true man Jesus.

Everywhere there are signs that point to the sex god:
    Books declare that sex is our savior;
    Songs are sung as prayers to sex;
    Pictures show its airbrushed incantations;
    Advertisers hawk its perfume and after-shave
    libations.
Help me know that sex is not salvation.
Help me see instead that there is salvation for sex.
For the exciting sensations of erotic love,
    I offer you my thanks.
For the affirmation of self-giving love,
    I offer you my thanks.
Lord, you replace sexual boredom with joy;
    you point past sexual slavery to the hope of
    purity;
    you enable sexual lovers to be friends;
    you teach how to replace lust-making with love-
    making.
Would I have any hope for sexual responsibility
Without the power you give?
Would I ever be a covenant keeper
Without the fidelity you inspire?
Thank you, Lord, for a love that stays when the bed
    is made.
Help me to keep my marriage bed undefiled—
    To see it as an altar of grace and pleasure.
Keep sex good in my life,
    Through your redeeming love.
Teach me to say:
    "Thank God for sex!"[10]

Notes

1. Harry Hollis, Jr., *Thank God for Sex* (Nashville, TN: Broadman Press, 1975), pp. 11-12. Used by permission.
2. Lewis B. Smedes, *Sex for Christians* (Grand Rapids, MI: Wm. B. Eerdmans Publishing Co., 1976), pp. 15-16.
3. Letha Scanzoni, *Sex Is a Parent Affair* (Ventura, CA: Regal, 1973), adapted from pp. 18-21.
4. Hollis, *Thank God for Sex*, pp. 56-57. Used by permission.
5. Dwight Small, *Christian Celebrate Your Sexuality* (Old Tappan, NJ: Fleming H. Revell Co., 1974), p. 190.
6. David L. Luecke, *The Relationship Manual* (Columbia, MD: The Relationship Institute, 1981), p. 63.
7. Helen Singer Kaplan, *Disorders of Sexual Desire* (New York: Simon and Schuster, 1979), p. 6.
8. James Halperna and Mark Sherman, *Afterplay* (Briarcliff Manor, NY: Stein and Day, 1979).
9. Dr. Ed Wheat, *Love Life* (Grand Rapids, MI: Zondervan Publications, 1980), pp. 76-77.
10. Hollis, *Thank God for Sex*, pp. 109-111. Used by permission.

~TEN~
Creative Ways to Keep Your Romance Alive

*O*ne of the most important keys to keeping romance alive is the freshness and creativity of your romantic approach. Even your most romantic "move" becomes old and ineffective if it's the only technique you use. Trying new methods of communicating and acting out your love will help keep the excitement level high in your marriage.

I'm sure you have many creative ideas for romance. In fact, I would love to know what you and your mate consider romantic! But now and then you may need to reach outside your own idea bank for some new romantic strategies. Consider the suggestions in this chapter and don't be afraid to be adventuresome with your spouse. Try several of these ideas—you may find new dimensions of romance just waiting to be uncovered!

Ideas for Romantic Activities

1. *The Sounds of Romance.* Find out what sounds are most soothing

and romantic to your spouse and surprise him or her occasionally by providing them. Secure a recording of a favorite romantic song to play on the stereo. As I mentioned earlier, Joyce and I enjoy holding hands and listening to John Denver records as we gaze at our miniature forest and waterfall. There are also some romantic videos, which are not X-rated, that you can rent or purchase.

Thanks to the marvels of electronic technology there are other sounds available today that you can use to create a romantic atmosphere. Mailing addresses are included for many of these suggestions, but you may also want to check your local record store, which may carry a comparable selection. Recorded waterfall sounds with piano and violin background is available from Global Pacific Distributors, Box 1784, Kamuela, HI 96743. Sound effects records from radio and television can be obtained from Major Records, Thomas J. Valentino, Inc., 151 W. 46th Street, New York, NY 10036.

"Desert Dawn Song" is an original composition by some musicians who have lived in the desert. Bird sounds and instruments are found on an edition that is available from Soundings of the Planet, P.O. Box 43512, Tucson, AZ 85733. There are also a number of programs featuring the sounds of nature which can provide romantic background to a peaceful evening at home. Some titles are "English Meadow," "Sounds of the Surf," "Canoe to Loon Lake" and "Redwood Forest Trail." Write to the Nature Company, Box 2310, Berkeley, CA 94702 (1-800-227-1114).

If you were raised during the 40s, 50s or 60s, there may be several "oldies but goodies" records that will bring back romantic memories. Check with the following companies for listings of songs from the decade you enjoy: American Pie, P.O. Box 66455, Dept. 405, Los Angeles, CA 90066; House of Oldies, 35 Carmine St., New York, NY 11014; Aardvark Music, Box 69441, Los Angeles, CA 90069; The Record Hunter, Mail Order Department, 507 Fifth Avenue, New York, NY 10017.

2. *Name a Star.* Did you know you can actually name a star after your spouse? What a great way to express your love! You can official-

ly designate one of God's stars to your life-long partner. There are also binary stars, a celestial pair orbiting together, that you could name for the two of you. When you have a star named for your spouse, you will receive an embossed certificate, two star-spangled charts noting the star's location in the galaxy, and a booklet about stars. And your star's name is registered in the International Star Registry's Swiss vault. All the names are cataloged in the book, *Your Place in the Cosmos.* For information write to International Star Registry, 1821 Willow Road, Northfield, IL 60093.

3. *Old Romantic Classics.* Some of the best romantic movies are old classics from the 30s and 40s. Check with your local video store for cassette versions you can enjoy during a romantic evening at home. You may also write to Blackhawk Films, One Eagle Brewery, Box 3990, Davenport, IA 52808 or Video Yesteryear, Box C, Sandy Hook, CT 06482.

4. *Recorded Invitation.* Invite your spouse to a romantic activity or interlude by means of a message on cassette tape. Practice your message and your delivery. Then play some romantic background music as you record your message. Use your most romantic and inviting tone of voice and inflections. Be sure to label or preface the recording, "For your ears only!"

5. *Computerized Love Letters.* Do you need help creating a love letter? There is a software program available called *Babble 123* that will write your love letter for you. The letters can be written in three different tones: flaming passion, friendly or fading fast. Check your local software store or write to Fairfield Software, 1900 W. Stone, Fairfield, IA 52556.

6. *Valentine Variations.* You can order Valentine greetings from the past by writing to: Yesterday's Paper, Inc., Paper Antiques, Box 294, Naperville, IL 60566. Also, Cupid by Mail is a service that will send your spouse a Valentine card from you on each of the six days before Valentine's Day. For more information write to Greetings and Salutations, 320 King Street, Alexandria, VA 22314.

7. *Dial-a-Gift.* You can send your spouse a gift for no special occa-

sion from Dial-a-Gift. This company creates gift packages such as a basket full of candy kisses anchoring a bear-shaped balloon. You can also custom design your own gift package. Write: Dial-a-Gift, 2265 E. 4800 St., Salt Lake City, UT 84117.

8. *Banner-gram.* Send your partner a gigantic banner-gram. You decide on the message and the time and place of delivery. Your message will be inscribed on the 15-foot banner. I have used this service on several occasions. You can mail your order to Computer Greetings Corporation, 22019 Vanowen St., Suite K, Canoga Park, CA 91303. Also check your local quick print shop, which may offer this service.

9. *Personalized Love.* You can show your love by replacing the labels on your clothes (or your spouse's) with a custom-made label bearing your name (or your spouse's). For labels write to ABAT Printed Novelties, 130 W. 29th St., New York, NY 10001.

Many states allow for personalized license plates. I've seen many in California which range from a couple's initials to I LUV JO, etc. Check with your motor vehicles department or automobile club for information.

10. *Love Letter Ghostwriter.* Create your own love letter with some personalized assistance. Cyrano's Quill is not a computer, but writing-oriented people who will take your ideas and create a beautiful love letter for you. Write to Cyrano's Quill, P.O. Box 1771, Clifton, NJ 07015. Or if you prefer your message written as poetry, write to Cyrano's Poems at the same address.

11. *Love Message Poster.* Once I obtained a mechanized poster advertising Hawaiian Punch from a market. Using my own materials I converted the poster into a personalized message. Check with the manager of your local market or drug store about available posters you could use. You can also make a love message collage of cut-outs from magazines. Use the collage to invite your spouse on a date, say "I love you," etc.

12. *Picture Poster.* Give your mate a giant-sized poster of yourself. Many photo stores offer the service of blowing up ordinary snapshots to poster size. Also check the classified ads in the back pages of mag-

azines for photo services advertised there. You can also order a monthly calendar with your picture on it from Jet Color Lab, P.O. Box 9888, Seattle, WA 98109.

13. *Romantic Party Kit.* Yes, there are sources for romantic party supplies. For a "Valentine Fling" kit, with balloons, Cupids, cutouts, etc., contact Paradise Products, P.O. Box 568, El Cerrito, CA 94530. Another distributor of party supplies is Paper East—The Party Store, 866 Lexington Avenue, New York, NY 10021.

14. *Romantic Postmark.* What's in a name? Plenty! Have you ever sent a love letter or special gift from a romantic sounding location like Bridal Veil, OR 97010, Loveland, CO 80537, Loving, NM 88256, Romance, WV 25175, or Valentine, NE 69201? A postmark from one of these locations can add just the right touch of romance to a letter or card. Seal your message in its envelope, stamp it and address it to your mate. Then place your envelope in a larger envelope and address it to the postmaster in the town of your choice. Include a note asking that your envelope be hand stamped and mailed from that post office. You may find additional locations to fit your purposes by checking a ZIP code directory in the post office.

15. *Borrowed Letters and Poems.* Have you ever browsed through the volumes of poetry at the public library? You will find many romantic poems that you may want to read aloud to your mate. Also you may want to look for published collections of love letters to read or provide you with ideas for your own compositions. Here are a few suggestions: *Famous Love Letters* by Marjorie Bowen (Falcraft, 1978), *An Anthology of Love Letters* by Lady Antonia Fraser (Knopf, 1977) and *The Love Letters of William and Mary Wordsworth* compiled by Cornell University Press. Just recently I found a book with a collection of love poems edited by Susan Schutz. It's called *You Mean So Much to Me* and is available from Blue Mountain Press, P.O. Box 4549, Boulder, CO 80306.

16. *Flag Day.* On Memorial Day or Veterans' Day we often see United States flags flying from many of the homes in our neighborhood. Create your own large flag for your spouse's birthday, anniversary or Valentine's Day and fly it for everyone to see. Check with professional

flag or banner manufacturers, or purchase your own materials and design your own masterpiece.

17. *Communicate with Chocolate.* Some say that chocolate produces a "high" similar to the experience of falling in love. Chocolate does contain a chemical component like one which the brain releases when one is infatuated. I'm not saying that chocolate is an aphrodisiac, but it is a tasty treat that makes a welcome gift.

Believe it or not, you can purchase a chocolate letter, including up to 80 letters engraved on a half-pound block of chocolate, gift packaged and shipped to your mate. Write to The Chocolate Letter, 130 W. 72nd St., New York, NY 10023. Chocolate greeting cards, including "I love you," are available from Astor Chocolate Corp., 4825 Metropolitan Avenue, Glendale, NY 11385.

Send a chocolate jigsaw puzzle to your loved one. It is white chocolate with dark chocolate design of Cupid figures, hearts, bows and arrows and a message. Plan a private picnic for the two of you in your bedroom or at a special hideaway. Or save this treat for a special surprise on your vacation. Order from the Chocolate Catalogue GL-1, 3983 Gratiot, St. Louis, MO 63110.[1]

18. *Creative Hugging.* Make and decorate copies of the Hug Party invitation (see next page) and give them to your spouse periodically.[2]

19. *Appointment for Romance.* If your spouse uses an appointment calendar at work, schedule yourself into his/her day by using a phony name. Bring a picnic lunch or snack, or take your mate out to lunch or coffee break. Or if time is limited, just stay a few minutes for hugs, kisses and words of love and encouragement.

20. *Love Prescription.* Go to your local pharmacy and purchase at least 30 empty prescription capsules and an empty pill bottle. Using different colored paper, write 30 tiny notes to your spouse, roll them up and insert each note in a capsule. Place the capsules in the bottle and label it "Take one each day for a month." (You may be able to talk the pharmacist into typing your "prescription" on an official pharmacy label and attaching it to the bottle for an authentic look!) The notes can range from "I love you" messages to "coupons" for three kisses, lunch

You're Invited to a Hug Party Because:

♥ *You're the world's greatest hugger*
♥ *It wouldn't be a party without you*
♥ *You'll stay and help clean up*
♥ *Someday you'll be rich and famous*
♥ *My mother asked me to*
♥ *You're so huggable and cuddly*
♥ *If you hug so will everyone else*
♥ *You're my hug therapist*
♥ *It's at your place*
♥ *You're my main squeeze*
♥ *The all-new Hug Army wants you!*
♥ *I like you*
♥ *We could all use a few more hugs*
♥ *You give great hugs*

Please try to make it.
R.S.V.P.

in the backyard, dinner out at your favorite restaurant, an hour of bedroom romance, etc. Be creative! Give the filled bottle to your spouse for a special occasion or just as a "no special occasion" treat.

Guidelines for Romantic Getaways

Here are several practical tips for those special occasions when just the two of you can get away from the house for a few hours or a few days.

1. *Plan Ahead Together.* When planning a getaway, write ahead to the local chamber of commerce, hotels or resorts for brochures. Obtain information on your destination from a travel agent or your automobile club. Look over the brochures together and fantasize about your getaway, even if you will only be gone for one night. Plan your itinerary and schedule together. The planning, dreaming and anticipating will boost your enjoyment of the event. If the getaway is a surprise for your spouse, the anticipation is yours but the enjoyment will be mutually shared.

2. *Use Discount Books.* One way to save money on getaways is to use discount books. For example, each year I order an Entertainment book for the Orange County area of Southern California. Since Joyce and I enjoy eating out on many of our dates, the Entertainment book is a real money saver. The book contains coupons offering two meals for the price of one at 75 to 100 different restaurants. It was through the Entertainment book that we discovered a very romantic restaurant located only three miles from our home. We have frequented the restaurant for more than eight years. There are also coupons for 50 percent discounts at many hotels.

Entertainment books are available for about 30 cities in the U.S. When Joyce and I plan a getaway of three or four days to one of these cities, I will order a local discount book for our dining and some amusements. Entertainment books may be obtained from Entertainment, P.O. Box 770, New York, NY 10960-0770. One word of warning, however: Don't scrimp too much on a romantic getaway. You are investing in your marriage!

3. *Communicate Your Preferences.* If your getaway will take you to a resort, hotel or motel that is new to you, be sure to let the staff know of your special needs and wants, likes and dislikes. Do you want a room with a view, quiet room or non-smoking room? Would you enjoy a fireplace, Jacuzzi or hot tub? Do you prefer king-size bed, water bed or bunk beds? Attention to these details will make your getaway even more special.

4. *Cover Details at Home.* Think through and plan for all the details of baby-sitting, pet care, and mail and newspaper pickup *before* you leave so you don't need to think about them while you are gone. Make a list of what needs to be done beforehand as well as important tasks that will need your attention when you return. Some couples even use a preplanned getaway checklist. If one of you is Mr. or Mrs. Super-checker-upper, write yourself a note assuring that you have checked up on everything at least twice!

Now that our children are out of the home, Joyce and I no longer need a baby-sitter when we get away. But we do need a combination house sitter and pet sitter to care for one Sheltie, one cat, 200 tropical fish, and a golden retriever—at last count!

5. *Establish Ground Rules.* There are some things that should be excluded from a romantic getaway. A list of mutually agreed upon ground rules may help set the stage for the romantic atmosphere you're getting away for. No talking about work or the children. No talking about conflicts, in-laws, bills, or other irritating topics. Don't worry about staying on diets. Do not take briefcases or make phone calls to the office. Take along recreational reading only. Make a commitment to unplug the TV while you are there. Yes, you read me correctly. Unplug the television even if major sports events are on!

6. *Don't Overplan.* Allow gaps in your getaway schedule to relax and loaf and talk and love. Practice spontaneity.

7. *Emergencies Only.* If you are going away for several days, tell your friends and relatives that you don't want to hear from them unless an emergency arises. And be sure to define what you mean by an emergency.

8. *Spread the Word.* Tell everyone you meet on your outing—hotel clerks, waiters, bellhops—that this is one of your romantic getaways. You'll be surprised how many people will do their best to help you enjoy your special event.

9. *Pray Together.* Set aside special times for prayer, perhaps focusing your prayer on thankfulness for your sexual relationship as suggested in chapter 9. Read portions of the Song of Solomon aloud to each other for your devotions.

10. *Share Love Words.* Tell each other how much you love one another using many thoughtful and creative approaches. Share your romantic memories together—a favorite getaway in the past, a memorable card or letter, an outstanding lovemaking interlude you recall. Also plan what you are going to share with friends and family when they ask you where you went on your getaway and what you did. Again, be creative!

11. *Read a Love Poem.* On one of your romantic getaways (which could be in your own home), set aside time to read one of the most romantic love poems ever written. "The Most Beautiful Love Song Ever Written," an adaptation of the Song of Solomon, is presented here:

"The Most Beautiful Love Song Ever Written"

Shulamith's First Days in the Palace (1:2-11)

The King's fiancée, Shulamith, in soliloquy

How I wish he would shower me with kisses for his exquisite kisses are more desirable than the finest wine. The gentle fragrance of your cologne brings the enchantment of springtime. Yes, it is the rich fragrance of your heart that awakens my love and respect. Yes, it is your character that brings you admiration from every girl of the court. How I long for you to come take me with you to run and laugh through the countryside of this kingdom. (You see, the King had brought me to the kingdom's palace.)

Women of the court to the King

We will always be very thankful and happy because of you, O King. For we love to speak of the inspiring beauty of your love.

Shulamith in soliloquy

They rightly love a person like you, my King.

Shulamith to women of the court

I realize that I do not display the fair and delicate skin of one raised in the comfort of a palace. I am darkened from the sun—indeed, as dark as the tents of the humble desert nomads I used to work beside. But now I might say that I am also as dark as the luxurious drapery of the King's palace. Nevertheless, what loveliness I do have is not so weak that the gaze of the sun should make it bow its head in shame. And if the glare of the sun could not shame me, please know that neither will the glare of your contempt. I could not help it that my stepbrothers were angry with me and demanded that I work in the vineyard they had leased from the King. It was impossible for me to care for it and for the vineyard of my own appearance.

Shulamith to King

Please tell me, you whom I love so deeply, where you take your royal flock for its afternoon rest. I don't want to search randomly for you, wandering about like a woman of the streets.

Women of the court to Shulamith

If you do not know, O fairest among women, why not simply go ahead and follow the trail of the flocks, and then pasture your flock beside the shepherds' huts?

King to Shulamith

Your presence captivates attention as thoroughly as a single mare among a hundred stallions. And how perfectly your lovely jewelry and necklace adorn your lovely face.

Women of the court to Shulamith

We shall make even more elegant necklaces of gold and silver to adorn her face.

In a Palace Room (1:12-14)

Shulamith in soliloquy

While my King was dining at his table, my perfume refreshed me with its soothing fragrance. For my King is the fragrance and my thoughts of him are like a sachet of perfume hung around my neck, over my heart, continually refreshing me. How dear he is to me, as dear as the delicate henna blossoms in the oasis of En-Gedi. What joy I have found in that oasis!

In the Countryside (1:15—2:7)

King to Shulamith

You are so beautiful, my love. You are so beautiful. Your soft eyes are as gentle as doves.

Shulamith to King

And you are handsome, my love, and so enjoyable. It's so wonderful to walk through our home of nature together. Here the cool grass is a soft couch to lie upon, to catch our breath and to gaze at the beams and rafters of our house—the towering cedars and cypresses all around. Lying here I feel like a rose from the valley of Sharon, the loveliest flower in the valley.

King to Shulamith

Only the loveliest flower in the valley? No, my love. To me you are like a flower among thorns compared with any other woman in the world.

Shulamith to King

And you, my precious King, are like a fruitful apple tree among the barren trees of the forest compared with all the men in the world.

Shulamith in soliloquy

No longer do I labor in the heat of the sun. I find cool rest in the shade of this apple tree. Nourishment from its magical fruit brings me the radiant health only love brings. And he loves me so much. Even when he brings me to the great royal banquets attended by the most influential people in this kingdom and beyond, he is never so concerned for them that his love and his care for me is not as plain as a royal banner lifted high above my head.

How dear he is to me! My delightful peace in his love makes me so weak from joy that I must rest in his arms for strength. Yet such loving comfort makes me more joyful and weaker still. How I wish he could lay me down beside him and embrace me! But how important it is I promise, with the gentle gazelles and deer of the countryside as my witnesses, not to attempt to awaken love until love is pleased to awaken itself.

On the Way to the Countryside (2:8-17)

Shulamith in soliloquy

I hear my beloved. Look! He is coming to visit. And he is as dashing as a young stag leaping upon the mountains, springing upon the hills. There he is, standing at the door, trying to peer through the window and peep through the lattice. At last he speaks.

King to Shulamith

Come, my darling, my fair one, come with me. For look, the winter has passed. The rain is over and gone. The blossoms have appeared in the land. The time of singing has come, and the voice of the turtledove has been heard in the land. The fig tree has ripened its figs, and the vines in blossom have given forth fragrance. Let us go, my darling, my lovely one; come along with me. O my precious, gentle dove. You have been like a dove in the clefts of the mountain rocks, in the hidden places along the mountain trails. Now come out from the hidden place and let me see you. Let me hear the coo of your voice. For your voice is sweet and you are as gracefully beautiful as a dove in flight silhouetted against a soft blue sky. My love, what we have together is a valuable treasure; it is like a garden of the loveliest flowers in the world. Let us promise each other to catch any foxes that could spoil our garden when now at long last it blossoms for us.

Shulamith in soliloquy

My beloved belongs to me and I belong to him—this tender King who grazes his flock among the lilies.

Shulamith to the King

How I long for the time when all through the night, until the day takes its first breath and the morning shadows flee from the sun, that you, my beloved King, might be a gazelle upon the hills of my breasts.

Shulamith Waits for Her Fiancé (3:1-5)

Shulamith in soliloquy

How I miss the one I love so deeply. I could not wait to see him. I thought to myself, "I must get up and find him. I will get up now and look around the streets and squares of the city for him. Surely I'll be able to find this one I love so much." But I could not find him. When the night watchmen of the city found me, I immediately asked them if they had seen this one I loved so deeply. But they had not. Yet no sooner did I pass from them than I found my beloved.

I held on and on and would not let him go until I could bring him to my home. I still held on until my fearful anxieties left me and I felt peaceful once again. How hard it is to be patient! You women of the court, we must promise ourselves, by the gazelles and deer of the field, not to awaken love until love is pleased to awaken itself.

The Wedding Day (3:6-11)

Poet

What can this be coming from the outskirts of the city like columns of smoke, perfumed clouds of myrrh and frankincense, clouds of the scented powders of the merchant? Look! It is the royal procession with Solomon carried upon his lavish couch by his strongest servants. And take a look at all those soldiers around it! That is the imperial guard, the sixty mightiest warriors in the entire kingdom. Each one is an expert with his weapon and valiant in battle. Yet now each one has a sword at his side only for the protection of the King and his bride. Look at the luxurious couch Solomon is carried on. He has had it made especially for this day. He made its frame from the best timber of Lebanon. Its posts are made of silver, its back of gold, and its seat of royal purple cloth. And do you see its delicate craftsmanship! It reflects the skill of the women of the court who gave their best work out of love for the King and his bride. Let us all go out and look upon King Solomon wearing his elegant wedding crown. Let us go out and see him on the most joyful day of his life.

The Wedding Night (4:1—5:1)

King to Shulamith

You are so beautiful, my love, you are so beautiful. Your

soft eyes are as gentle as doves from behind your wedding veil. Your hair is as captivating as the flowing movement of a flock descending a mountain at sunset. Your full and lovely smile is as cheerful and sparkling as pairs of young lambs scurrying up from a washing. And only a thread of scarlet could have outlined your lips so perfectly. Your cheeks flush with the redness of the pomegranate's hue. Yet you walk with dignity and stand with the strength of a fortress. Your necklace sparkles like the shields upon the fortress tower. But your breasts are as soft and gentle as fawns grazing among lilies. And now at last, all through the night—until the day takes it first breath and the morning shadows flee from the sun—I will be a gazelle upon the hills of your perfumed breasts. You are completely and perfectly beautiful, my love, and flawless in every way. Now bring your thoughts completely to me, my love. Leave your fears in the far away mountains and rest in the security of my arms.

You excite me, my darling bride; you excite me with but a glance of your eyes, with but a strand of your necklace. How wonderful are your caresses, my beloved bride. Your love is more sweetly intoxicating than the finest wine. And the fragrance of your perfume is better than the finest spices. The richness of honey and milk is under your tongue, my love. And the fragrance of your garments is like the fragrance of the forests of Lebanon.

You are a beautiful garden fashioned only for me, my darling bride. Yes, like a garden kept only for me. Or like a fresh fountain sealed just for me. Your garden is overflowing with beautiful and delicate flowers of every scent and color. It is a paradise of pomegranates with luscious fruit, with henna blossoms and nard, nard and saffron, calamus and cinnamon with trees of frankincense, myrrh and aloes with all the choicest of spices. And you are pure as fresh water, yet more than a mere fountain. You are a spring for many gardens—a well of life-giving water. No, even more, you are like the fresh streams flowing from Lebanon which give life to the entire countryside.

Shulamith to King

Awake, O north wind, and come, wind of the south. Let your breezes blow upon my garden and carry its fragrant spices to my beloved. May he follow the enchanting spices to my garden and come in to enjoy its luscious fruit.

King to Shulamith

I have rejoiced in the richness of your garden, my darling bride. I have been intoxicated by the fragrance of your myrrh and perfume. I have tasted the sweetness of your love like honey. I have enjoyed the sweetness of your love like an exquisite wine and the refreshment of your love like the coolness of milk.

Poet to couple

Rejoice in your lovemaking as you would rejoice at a great feast, O lovers. Eat and drink from this feast to the fullest. Drink, drink and be drunk with one another's love.

A Problem Arises (5:2—6:3)

Shulamith in soliloquy

I was half asleep when I heard the sound of my beloved husband knocking gently upon the door of our palace chamber. He whispered softly, "I'm back from the countryside, my love, my darling, my perfect wife." My only answer was a mumbled, "I've already gone to sleep, my dear." After all, I had already prepared for bed. I had washed my face and put on my old nightgown.

But then my beloved gently opened the door and I realized I really wanted to see him. I had hesitated too long though. By the time I arose to open the door, he had already walked away, leaving only a gift of my favorite perfume as a reminder of his love for me. Deep within my heart I was reawakened to my love for him. It was just that the fatigue and distractions of the day had brought my hesitating response. I decided to try to find him. I threw on my clothes, went outside the palace and began to call out to him.

But things went from bad to worse. The night watchmen of the city mistook me for a secretive criminal sneaking about in the night. They arrested me in their customarily rough style, then jerking my shawl from my head they saw the face of their newly found suspect—a "great" police force we have!

O, you women of the court, if you see my beloved King, please tell him that I deeply love him, that I am lovesick for him.

Women of the court to Shulamith

What makes your husband better than any other, O fairest of women? What makes him so great that you request this so fervently of us?

Shulamith to women of the court

My beloved husband is strikingly handsome, the first to be noticed among ten thousand men. When I look at him, I see a face with a tan more richly golden than gold itself. His hair is as black as a raven's feathers and as lovely as palm leaves atop the stately palm tree. When I look into his eyes, they are as gentle as doves peacefully resting by streams of water. They are as pure and clear as health can make them.

When he places his cheek next to mine, it is as fragrant as a garden of perfumed flowers. His soft lips are as sweet and scented as lilies dripping with nectar. And how tender are his fingers like golden velvet when he touches me! He is a picture of strength and vitality. His stomach is as firm as a plate of ivory rippling with sapphires. And his legs are as strong and elegant as alabaster pillars set upon pedestals of fine gold. His appearance is like majestic Mt. Lebanon, prominent with its towering cedars.

But beyond all this, the words of his heart are full of charm and delight. He is completely wonderful in every way. This is the one I love so deeply, and this is the one who is my closest friend, O women of the palace court.

Women of the court to Shulamith

Where has your beloved gone, then, O fairest among women? Where has he gone? We will help you find him.

Shulamith to women of the court

Oh, I know him well enough to know where he has gone. He likes to contemplate as he walks through the garden and cares for his special little flock among the lilies. I know him, for I belong to him and he belongs to me—this gentle shepherd who pastures his flock among the lilies.

The Problem Resolved (6:4-13)

King to Shulamith

My darling, did you know that you are as lovely as the city of Tirzah glittering on the horizon of night? No, more than that you are as lovely as the fair city of Jerusalem. Your beauty is as breathtaking as scores of marching warriors. (No, do not look at me like that now, my love; I have more to tell you.)

Do you remember what I said on our wedding night? It is still just as true. Your hair is as captivating as the flowing movement of a flock descending a mountain at sunset. Your lovely smile is as cheerful and sparkling as pairs of young lambs scurrying up from a washing. And your cheeks still flush with the redness of the pomegranate's hue.

King in soliloquy

The palace is full of its aristocratic ladies and dazzling mistresses belonging to the noblemen of the court. But my lovely wife, my dove, my flawless one, is unique among them all. And these ladies and mistresses realize it too. They too must praise her. As we approached them in my chariot, they eventually perceived that we were together again.

Women of the court to one another

Who is that on the horizon like the dawn, now fair as the moon but now plain and bright as the sun and as majestic as scores of marching warriors?

Shulamith in the chariot in soliloquy

I went down to the garden where I knew my King would be. I wanted to see if the fresh flowers and fruits of spring had come. I wanted to see if our reunion might bring a new season of spring love for my husband and me. Before I knew what happened, we were together again and riding past the palace court in his chariot. I can still hear them calling out, "Return, return O Shulamith; return that we may gaze at the beloved wife of the King."

King to Shulamith

How they love to look upon the incomparable grace and beauty of a queen.

In the Royal Bedroom (7:1-10)

King to Shulamith

How delicate are your feet in sandals, my royal prince's daughter! The curves of your hips are as smooth and graceful as the curves of elegant jewelry, perfectly fashioned by the skillful hands of a master artist. As delectable as a feast of wine and bread is your stomach—your navel is like the goblet of wine, and your stomach is the soft warm bread. Your breasts are as soft and gentle as fawns grazing among lilies, twins of a gazelle, and your neck is smooth as ivory to the touch. Your eyes are as peaceful as the pools of water in the valley of Heshbon, near the gate of the populous city.

Yet how strong you walk in wisdom and discretion. You are, indeed, as majestically beautiful as Mt. Carmel. Your long flowing hair is as cool and soft as silken threads draped round my neck, yet strong enough to bind me as your captive forever. How lovely and delightful you are, my dear, and how especially delightful is your love! You are as graceful and splendrous as a palm tree silhouetted against the sky. Yes, a palm tree—and your breasts are its luscious fruit.

I think I shall climb my precious palm tree and take its tender fruit gently into my hand. O my precious one, let your breasts be like the tender fruit to my taste, and now let me kiss you and breathe your fragrant breath. Let me kiss you and taste a sweetness better than wine.

Shulamith to King

And savor every drop, my lover, and let its sweetness linger long upon your lips, and let every drop of this wine bring a peaceful sleep.

Shulamith in soliloquy

I belong to my beloved husband and he loves me from the depths of his soul.

In the Countryside (7:11—8:14)

Shulamith to King

Spring's magic flowers have perfumed the pastel countryside and enchanted the hearts of all lovers. Come, my precious lover; every delicious fruit of spring is ours for the taking. Let us return to our springtime cottage of towering cedars and cypresses where the plush green grass is its endless carpet and the orchards are its shelves for every luscious fruit. I have prepared a basketful for you, my love, to give you in a sumptuous banquet of love beneath the sky.

I wish we could pretend you were my brother, my real little brother. I could take you outside to play, and playfully kiss you whenever I wished. But then I could also take your hand and bring you inside and you could teach me and share with me your deep understanding of life. Then how I wish you would lay me down beside you and love me.

Shulamith to women of the court

I encourage you not to try to awaken love until love is pleased to awaken itself. How wonderful it is when it blossoms in the proper season.

Shulamith to King

Do you remember where our love began? Under the legendary sweetheart tree, of course, where every love begins and grows and then brings forth a newborn child, yet not without the pain of birth. Neither did our love begin without the pain, the fruitful pain of birth. O, my darling lover, make me your most precious possession held securely in your arms, held close to your heart. True love is as strong and irreversible as the onward march of death. True love never ceases to care, and it would no more give up the beloved than the grave would give up the dead.

The fires of true love can never be quenched because the source of its flame is God himself. Even were a river of rushing water to pass over it, the flame would yet shine forth. Of all the gifts in the world, this priceless love is the most precious and possessed only by those to whom it is freely given. For no man could purchase it with money, even the richest man in the world.

King to Shulamith

Do you remember how it was given to us?

Shulamith to King

My love, I truly believe I was being prepared for it long before I even dreamed of romance. I remember hearing my brothers talking one evening. It was shortly after my father died, and they were concerned to raise me properly, to prepare me for the distant day of marriage. They were like a roomful of fathers debating about what to do with their only daughter. They finally resolved simply to punish and restrict me if I were promiscuous but to reward and encourage me if I were chaste. How thankful I am that I made it easy for them. I could see even when I was very young that I wanted to keep myself for the one dearest man in my life.

And then you came. And everything I ever wanted I found in you. There I was, working daily in the vineyard my brothers had leased from you. And you "happened" to pass by and see me. That's how our love began.

I remember when I worked in that vineyard that a thousand dollars went to you and two hundred dollars for the ones taking care of its fruit for you. Now I am your vineyard, my lover, and I gladly give the entire thousand dollars of my worth to you; I give myself completely, withholding nothing of my trust, my thoughts, my care, my love. But my dear King, let us not forget that two hundred dollars belongs to the ones who took care of the fruit of my vineyard for you. How thankful we must be to my family who helped prepare me for you.

King to Shulamith

My darling, whose home is the fragrant garden, everyone listens for the sound of your voice, but let me alone hear it now.

Shulamith to King

Hurry, then, my beloved. And again be like a gazelle or young stag on the hills of my perfumed breasts.[3]

Notes

1. Resources and suggestions in this section are from several sources, including the author and participants in marriage enrichment seminars. Other ideas are adapted from the *Romantic Emporium* by Kennedy and Judy Babcock, (Kansas City, MO: Andrews, McMeel and Parker, 1986).
2. Adapted from Charles Farone, Philip Farone and Paul Planet, *Let's Hug* (Watertown, MA: Ivory Tower Publishing Co, 1985). Used by permission.
3. Taken from *A Song for Lovers* by S. Craig Glickman. 1976 by InterVarsity Christian Fellowship of the USA and used by permission of InterVarsity Press, P.O. Box 1400, Downers Grove, IL 60515.

Conclusion

*T*here's a phrase often used that talks about saving the best till last. In keeping with that axiom I want to leave you with two excellent resources that will enable you and inspire you to a life of love and romance with your mate.

The first resource identifies the single most important concept to the success of romancing your spouse. It is an exhortation that married couples of all ages must take to heart.

The Importance of Commitment

What will make the difference in the quality of your marriage? One word—commitment. One word? Yes, but a costly word that can bring tension and questions, and at the same time can bring peace, maturity, stability, continual love and romance.

Commit your life to the person of Jesus Christ, who is the Son of God. Commit your life to the Word of God, which brings stability and peace. Commit yourself to seeing your spouse as having such worth, value and dignity that God sent His Son to die for that person.

Commit your life as a couple to a life of prayer. There is no greater closeness and intimacy than when a couple opens their hearts to God together. Praying together enhances the completeness and oneness of a couple, while it puts their differences and adjustments in a better perspective.

Commit your life to giving your marriage top priority in terms of time, energy, thought and planning for growth. Commit your mind and thoughts toward creativity in loving your spouse and in becoming a caring creative lover. Commit yourself to a life of fidelity and faithfulness regardless of your feelings or the lure of the life around you.

Commit yourself and open yourself to the working of the Holy Spirit in your life. "But when the Holy Spirit controls our lives he will produce this kind of fruit in us: love, joy, peace, patience, kindness, goodness, faithfulness, gentleness and self-control" (Gal. 5:22-23, *TLB*).

Faith, hope and love will grow out of your commitment to one another and to God and His Word. May the following always be your prayer:

> Lord, we believe that You ordained marriage
> and that You also sustain it.
> Help us to exercise faith.
> Faith that You answer prayer
> and heal wounded hearts.
> Faith that You forgive and restore.
> Faith that Your hand of love
> will clasp our hands together.
> Faith that You build bridges of reconciliation.
> Faith that all things will work for good
> to those who love You.
> Help us to hold on to hope.
> Hope that enables us to endure
> times of trial and testing.
> Hope that fixes our gaze on possibilities
> rather than problems.
> Hope that focuses on the road ahead
> instead of detours already passed.
> Hope that instills trust, even in the midst of
> failure.
> Hope that harbors happiness.

Help us to lift up love.
Love that doesn't falter or faint
    in the wind of adversity.
Love that is determined to grow and bear
    fruit.
Love that is slow to anger and quick to
    praise.
Love that looks for ways of saying,
    "I care for you."
Love that remains steady during shaky
    days.
    Lord, may Your gifts of faith, hope and love find plenty of living room in our hearts. Thank You that these three abide—and the greatest is love. Make our home an outpost for Your kingdom and an oasis for wandering pilgrims. In the name of Jesus who blessed the marriage at Cana with a miracle. Amen.[1]

The Test of Time

Finally, here is an inspiring example of marital love and romance that has endured more than seven decades of marriage. Tracy Cabot tells the story and reveals the reasons for the success of couples she calls the survivors in marriage.

    How are the survivors different? They are bonded by their experiences and their memories. The memories of when things were better, the beautiful, happy times they've had together and even the memory of having survived the bad times.
    Of all the couples I talked to in my research, I was most impressed by Bob and Alberta. Their most shining example of married love is one I'll never forget.
    Bob and Alberta had just celebrated their seventy-third wedding anniversary when I interviewed them on their farm in

Washington. Bob, 93, and Alberta, 90, have nine children, nineteen grandchildren, and ten great-grandchildren.

Bob is mostly the silent type, but you can tell how much he adores Alberta. He's always touching her, hugging her, sneaking up and planting a kiss on her, even pinching her in the rear. Sometimes their kids are a little embarrassed by the lovey-dovey old folks, but I found myself wanting to make sure my husband and I stayed that excited and interested in each other when we're that old, so I listened carefully to Alberta's story.

"Our love was put to the test many times," she told me. "We went through the Depression together with four little children and no work to be found. Finally, we were forced to leave our farm in Oklahoma because of the dust storms and the long drought. We moved to Washington State with barely enough money to buy a decent meal.

"Most men would have panicked, but not my Bobby. He just tightened his belt and set about finding a job and working toward buying us another home. Women didn't have careers in those days, so I made my role as a homemaker my career. I was determined to be the best there was.

"Bobby didn't have to lift a finger when he came home from work, and I liked it that way. He worked long hard hours digging and hauling and making him happy was my job. I loved it and I know he respected me for it. He never took me for granted and he always treated me as if I was still his best girl."

Eventually, they bought a new farm, but life still wasn't easy. "With nine kids we didn't have a lot left over, but at least we could grow our food. It was hard for us to be alone, but Bobby didn't let that stop him from courting his girl, as he used to say.

"We couldn't afford to go anywhere, but we had a big farm and built-in baby-sitters with the older kids. We'd tell them we'd have to go out and sow, and then we'd go for long walks on our land. We'd picnic under our favorite oak tree near the Yakima River. And we'd make love there, giggling and whispering about what we'd do if the kids ever found us naked. They never did." Alberta's youngest daughter, 48, and divorced, told me she never knew until right then that's what her parents had been doing in the field all those times.

As they got older, and the ground got harder, and there got to be more money, Alberta and Bob would drive to the next town and check into a motel for a few hours, just to get away. "We'd get all excited. Just the way the desk clerk would look at us with no luggage and holding hands would get us all warm. In those days, doing something like that was rather naughty, and that made it even more fun.

"The next day I'd always find a huge bouquet of flowers on the dresser when I woke up. Bob picked them himself and there was always a note with the flowers. I saved the notes over the years, and whenever things were bad and one of the kids was sick or the crops failed, I'd bring out the notes he sent me with the flowers and we'd sit and read them together, and we'd always feel better."

Even today, with both Bob and Alberta in their nineties, they are so obviously in love that their children admit to being jealous, and curious about how they stay that way. Alberta let us in on her secrets one afternoon when Bob was out.

"I always let him know he's still the sexiest, most handsome man I've ever known," Alberta told me and her two daughters, as we sat in her real country kitchen.

Bob and Alberta's day is filled with lots of long hugs, hand squeezes and romantic cuddling. "It's cute: we think it's neat," say their grandchildren, even if Bob and Alberta's children think they're really an anomaly in today's world. In spite of that, several of Bob and Alberta's children confessed that they always compare their marriages to their parents' and often find them lacking. They wonder what it is their mother and father do that they don't do, how they kept their love alive through years of struggle. Alberta reminisced about how they stayed in love.

"Life has a way of sobering people up sometimes, but we stay young because we both have a good sense of humor. There've been times when I've been out of sorts about something, and I'll be doing the dishes and grumbling about something, and Bob will pop me on the rear with a dish towel.

"We're still very passionate," Alberta assured me. "Bob kisses me just the way he did when we were young. We hold hands when we walk down the street or when we just sit on the sofa watching television.

"We touch a lot. A squeeze of the hand can do so much to cheer a person up or just let them know you're there and you love them."[2]

Notes

1. James R. Bjorge, *Forty Ways to Say I Love You* (Minneapolis: Augsburg Publishing House, 1978), pp. 91-92. Reprinted by permission.
2. Tracy Cabot, *How to Keep a Man in Love with You Forever* (New York: McGraw-Hill Co., 1986), pp. 234-236. Reprinted by permission.

Exercises
and Quizzes for
Keeping Your
Romance Alive

On the following pages are some of the tests/exercises from the book that would be beneficial for you and/or your spouse to work through periodically. Keep track of your responses and track your progress—you'll find it exciting and worthwhile!

MARITAL INTIMACY CHECKUP[1]

(Instructions: After discussing each area, check the blanks
that apply to your relationship.)

Facts of Intimacy	Both Desire Improvement	Wife Desires Improvement	Husband Desires Improvement	Both Satisfied
1. Sexual Intimacy				
2. Emotional Intimacy (Being tuned to each other's wavelength)				
3. Intellectual Intimacy (Closeness in the world of ideas)				
4. Aesthetic Intimacy (Sharing in acts of creating beauty)				
5. Creative Intimacy (Sharing in acts of creating together)				
6. Recreational Intimacy (Relating in experiences of fun and play)				
7. Work Intimacy (Closeness of sharing common tasks)				
8. Crisis Intimacy (Closeness in coping with problems and pain)				
9. Conflict Intimacy (Facing and struggling with differences)				

Termites in Our Marriage

Take a few minutes and list what you think are some of the present or potential termites that could bring about a love recession in your marriage. Then list some from your spouse's perspective. After you have both completed the exercise, talk together about your lists.

From my perspective:	From my spouse's perspective:

"*Lover's Quotient Test*"

(This one was designed especially for the men—although it wouldn't hurt the wives to incorporate some of these suggestions, as well. Husbands, give yourself 10 points for each item on the following list if you have done it once in the past 6 months. If you have done any item on the list 2 or more times you get 20 points.)

☐ Have you phoned her during the week and asked her out for one evening that weekend without telling her where you are taking her? A mystery date.

☐ Have you gone parking with her at some safe and secluded spot and kissed and talked for an evening?

☐ Have you drawn a bath for her after dinner? Put a scented candle in the bathroom, add bath oil to the bath, send her there right after dinner, and then you clean up and put the kids to bed while she relaxes.

☐ Have you phoned her from work to tell her you were thinking nice thoughts about her?

☐ Have you written her a love letter and sent it special delivery?

☐ Have you made a tape recording of all the reasons you have for loving her? Give it to her wrapped in a sheer negligee!

☐ Have you given her a day off? You clean the house, fix the meals and take care of the kids.

☐ Have you put a special effects stereo recording of ocean waves on tape and played it while you had a nude luau on the living room floor? (If this seems a little far out for your tastes, you could substitute by either removing the stereo effects tape or having a popcorn party in the privacy of the bedroom instead.)

☐ Have you spent a whole evening (more than two hours) sharing mutual goals and planning family objectives with her and the children?

☐ Have you ever planned a surprise weekend? You make the reservations and arrange for someone to keep the children for two days. Tell her to pack her suitcase, but don't tell her where you are going. Make it someplace romantic.

☐ Have you picked up your clothes just one time in the past six months and put them on hangers?

☐ Have you given her an all-over body massage with scented lotion and a vibrator?

☐ Have you spent a session of making love to her that included at least two hours of romantic conversation, shared dreams, many positions of intercourse, and much variety of approach and caresses?

☐ Have you repaired something around the house which she has not requested?

☐ Have you kissed her passionately for at least 30 seconds one morning just before you left for work, or one evening when you walked in the door?

☐ Have you brought her an unexpected little gift like perfume, a ring, or an item of clothing?

☐ Have you replaced her old negligee?

How did you do? Have you improved since the first time you took this test? Let's check:

200-360—LOVER: You undoubtedly have one of the most satisfied wives in the country.

150-200—GOOD: Very few make this category.

100-150—AVERAGE: This husband is somewhat typical and usually not very exciting as a lover.

50-100—KLUTZ: Too many score in this category. I hope you'll begin to move up soon.

0-50—HUSBAND: There is a difference between a "husband" and a "lover." The only reason your wife is still married to you is that she's a Christian, she has unusual capacity for unconditional acceptance, and there are some verses in the Bible against divorce.[2]

Notes:
1. Howard J. Clinebell, Jr. and Charlotte H. Clinebell, *The Intimate Marriage* (San Francisco: Harper and Row Publishers, Inc., 1970), pp. 37-38.
2. Reprinted by permission of Thomas Nelson Publishers from the book *Solomon on Sex*, Copyright © 1977 by Joseph Dillow.

Study Questions for Individuals, Couples and Groups

Chapter 1

1. Thinking back on your expectations before marriage, name at least one romantic dream that has failed to come true. How do you feel about that? Do you think you were wrong to have expected it? Could you and/or your spouse have done more to make it come true?

2. What are some of the things you "learned" from your family of origin, as well as from cultural influences, to expect in the way of courtship and marriage customs? Now that you've been married for some time, do those customs still hold validity and purpose? Why or why not?

3. Referring back to the twelfth-century book *The Art of Courtly Love* by Andre the Chaplain, how many of our current romantic ideas are still influenced by the romantic ideas of that day, ideas that were based on infidelity and extramarital involvement? How do these ideas compare with the biblical view of love and marriage?

Study Questions...

4. What do you think of as the "ideal" romance? How much of your description is reflected in the theme of today's "happily-ever-after" romance novels? Why do you think these romance novels are so popular? Are these books just harmless entertainment? If not, what potential do you see for danger?
5. Reviewing the last four questions, how do you now view your overall expectations of romance? Are they realistic? Idealistic? Impossible? What can you do to bring your romantic expectations into line with reality, without giving up on romance altogether?

Chapter 2

1. Define romance in a personal way (one paragraph or less). What key words do you see in your description?
2. Did you do the exercise titled "Romance: A Novel Idea"? If so, what did you learn from it? How does what you wrote in the exercise compare with your definition of romance in question number 1?
3. In working through the exercise on "Romantic Fantasies and Facts," what did you learn about the stability of romantic fantasies? How have your romantic fantasies changed since you were a teenager?
4. Do you believe it is possible for romance to be present at all times in a marriage? Why or why not?
5. Can romantic experiences be planned or must they always be spontaneous? Is one type of romance (planned vs. spontaneous) better than the other?

Chapter 3

1. Define intimacy. In what ways is it the same and/or different from romance or love?
2. Does the thought of intimacy make you uncomfortable? Why or why not? How would your spouse answer this question?
3. How difficult is it for you to verbalize your feelings? How would your spouse answer this question?

4. Do you feel that you and your spouse have an open relationship, one where you can share your innermost feelings comfortably? How would you have answered that question when you were first married? How would you like to answer it in the future?

5. Do you and your husband pray together regularly? If not, how can you go about establishing this practice? If you already do, what benefits do you find in your relationship because of this practice?

Chapter 4

1. How did you react to the facts listed in the "Is It True Love?" section of this chapter? Did you disagree at any point? If so, why? Was there a time in your life when you believed differently from these facts? If so, what made you change your mind?

2. Did you and your spouse attend premarital counseling? If not, how do you think it might have benefited your marriage? If you did, how do you feel it has helped your marriage?

3. Did you locate yourself and your partner in the six basic love styles? Were you surprised at what you discovered? How can you use this knowledge to improve your relationship?

4. After reading the quotes in the section titled "A Loving Relationship," how would you answer the question, "What does it mean to love another person in terms of daily living?"

5. Define the word "commitment." How have you succeeded in living up to that definition in your marriage? In what areas do you see a need for improvement? What can you do to bring that improvement about?

Chapter 5

1. Can you think of at least three instances that had a negative effect on your romance? How could the negative effects of those instances be turned to something positive, even if these things happened a long time ago?

2. Before you married, do you think you knew your future spouse well enough to see him/her realistically, or were you "blinded" by love? How have the revelations of who your spouse really is affected your romantic feelings toward him/her?

3. What are some of the main changes/stages you have experienced in your marriage? In what ways have these changes affected you and your spouse similarly? differently?

4. What stage of marriage are you in now? Knowing what to expect in this stage, as well as in the stage to come, what adjustments will you make personally in order to help your transition from one stage to the next as a couple?

5. How can your relationship with Jesus Christ help you make these transitions? How can your relationship with Jesus Christ restore to your marital relationship some of the romance you may have lost in previous stages of your marriage?

Chapter 6

1. What are some of the "termites" that have eaten away at your romantic relationship? Be specific. Dig deep!

2. How many of these "termites" are offenses (either real or imagined) inflicted on you by your spouse? How many of them still need to be settled through forgiveness on your part?

3. When reading the section titled "Releasing Resentment," how many people, other than your spouse, did you discover that you still needed to forgive? Were you surprised at your discovery? Were you able to tie those long-lasting resentments in to your resentments toward your spouse?

4. When reading the section "Give a Positive Response," were you surprised to discover that your seemingly indifferent feelings toward certain people were really a state of emotional insulation? Were you able to dig down to the underlying resentment and then develop a positive response to eliminate that resentment? What did you discover about yourself during that exercise?

5. If you are still struggling with unforgiveness in some areas of your marriage, what can you do to help yourself separate your spouse from the hurt he/she inflicted on you so you can let that hurt go once and for all?

Chapter 7

1. Do you think it is possible for a couple to prevent love recessions in their marriage? Why or why not?
2. Are the negative results of a love recession irreversible? What can be done to redeem past losses from love recessions, as well as prevent future losses?
3. What are some of your favorite memories of nonsexual "touching" times in your life?
4. Are you a hugger by nature, or do you tend to pull away from this sort of greeting or show of affection? How much of this do you suppose is learned behavior (family of origin, cultural influences, etc.)? Do you see hugging as a healthy form of expressing affection? Why or why not?
5. What are some of the most creative dates you and your spouse have been on? What is your "dream date"? What would be your spouse's "dream date"?

Chapter 8

1. What was your first reaction to the statement, "You married a foreigner"? After reading the chapter, how do you feel about that statement now?
2. Name at least three times when you have presented an idea to your spouse, only to have him/her react negatively. How might presenting the idea in your spouse's "language" have changed his/her reaction?
3. Were you surprised when you discovered your love language? Your

spouse's? Have you tried adopting your spouse's language yet? If so, what were the results?

4. Now that you've read about visual, auditory and feelings people, to the best of your ability, list those closest to you (family, friends) in one of those three categories. How do you suppose adjusting your language style to theirs could affect your relationships? Are you willing to make those adjustments?

5. If possible, choose an item (or a scene or setting) and have your spouse describe it (written or verbally) as he/she believes you would describe it. Then you describe it yourself and compare notes. Reverse the process, and find out just how well you really know each other's language!

Chapter 9

1. Where did you gain your original ideas and feelings about sex (parents, friends, the Bible, etc.)? How did this chapter challenge some of your previous ideas about sex?

2. As you were growing up, who were your sexual role models? Were these healthy or unhealthy models? How did they affect your sexual growth? Do you have role models now (pastor and wife, etc.)? How does their relationship affect the way you think of sex within your own marriage?

3. Can you think of at least three negative attitudes you have had toward sex, either now or at some time in your life? How about three positive attitudes?

4. Since reading the chapter, have you and/or your spouse come up with at least one new way to improve your sexual relationship? How do you think your sexual relationship has changed since your honeymoon? Do you consider that change for the better or worse? Why?

5. How does your schedule (or that of your spouse) affect the quality of your sexual relationship? What changes could be made to improve the situation? Are you willing to make those changes?

Chapter 10

1. Of all the creative ideas listed in this chapter, which three do you think most appealed to your spouse? Why? Which three most appealed to you? Why?
2. Of all the creative ideas listed in this chapter, which three least appealed to your spouse? Why? Which three least appealed to you? Why?
3. What is the most creative way you have ever thought of to show love to your spouse? Did you follow through on it? Why or why not? If you did, what was his/her response?
4. What is the most creative way your spouse ever showed love to you? What was your reaction?
5. If money were no object, what would you do to show your love to your spouse today?